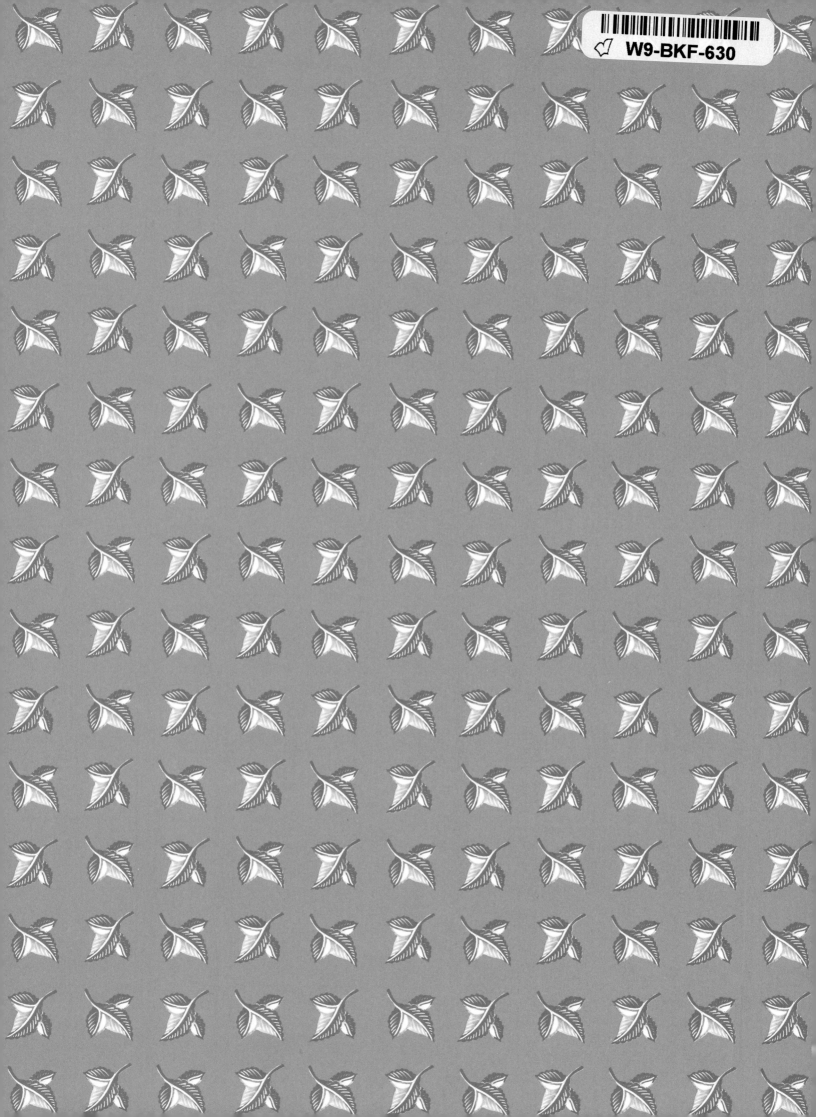

THE ULTIMATE
LOW CHOLESTEROL
LOW FAT COOKBOOK

CHRISTINE FRANCE

THE ULTIMATE
LOW CHOLESTEROL
LOW FAT COOKBOOK

CHRISTINE FRANCE

Over 220 delicious healthy recipes – step-by-step

ACROPOLIS BOOKS

First published by Lorenz Books in 1996
Reprinted in 1996
© 1996 Anness Publishing Limited

Lorenz Books is an imprint of
Anness Publishing Limited
Boundary Row Studios
1 Boundary Row
London SE1 8HP

This edition distributed in Canada by Book Express
an imprint of Raincoast Books Distribution Limited

ISBN 1 85967 237 X

A CIP catalogue record for this book
is available from the British Library

Publisher: Joanna Lorenz
Senior Cookery Editor: Linda Fraser
Assistant Editor: Emma Brown
Designer: Siân Keogh
Photographers: Karl Adamson, Steve Baxter,
James Duncan, Amanda Heywood and Don Last
Food for Photography: Carla Capalbo, Elizabeth Wolf-Cohen,
Wendy Lee and Jane Stevenson
Props Stylists: Madeleine Brehaut, Blake Minton,
Kirsty Rawlings and Fiona Tillet

Printed and bound in China

NOTES

For all recipes, quantities are given in both metric and imperial measures and,
where appropriate, measures are also given in standard cups and spoons. Follow
one set, but not a mixture because they are not interchangeable.

Standard spoon and cup measurements are level.
1 tbsp = 15ml, 1 tsp = 5ml, 1 cup = 250ml/8fl oz

Australian standard tablespoons are 20ml. Australian readers should use 3 tsp in
place of 1 tbsp for measuring small quantities of gelatine, cornflour, salt etc.

Size 3 (medium) eggs should be used unless otherwise stated.

CONTENTS

WHY A LOW FAT DIET?

We need a certain amount of fat in our diet for general health and it is a valuable source of energy. Also, it plays a vital role in making foods palatable to eat. However, most of us eat more fat than we need. You should not try to cut out fat altogether, but a lower fat diet has the benefits of weight loss and reduction in the risk of heart disease.

There are two types of fat – saturated and unsaturated. The unsaturated group includes two types – polyunsaturated and monounsaturated fats.

Saturated fats are the ones you should limit, as they increase cholesterol in the blood, and this can increase the risk of heart disease. The main sources of saturated fat are animal products such as dairy products and meat, but also hard fats and hydrogenated vegetable fat or oil. Polyunsaturated fats are essential in small quantities for good health, and are thought to help reduce the cholesterol in the blood. There is also some evidence that monounsaturated fats have a beneficial effect. The main sources of polyunsaturates are vegetable oils such as sunflower, corn and soya, and oily fish such as herring, mackerel, pilchards, sardines and trout. Sources of monounsaturated fats include olive, rapeseed and groundnut oils, as well as avocadoes and many nuts.

Cutting Down on Cholesterol?

Cholesterol is a substance which occurs naturally in the blood, and is essential for the formation of hormones, body cells, nerves and bile salts which help digestion.

A high cholesterol level can increase the likelihood of coronary heart disease, as it becomes deposited on the walls of the arteries, causing them to fur up. The main cause of raised cholesterol levels is eating too much fat, especially saturated fat. Eating too much saturated fat encourages the body to make more cholesterol than it needs, and also seems to prevent it getting rid of the excess.

The cholesterol found in foods such as egg yolk, offal, cheese, butter and shellfish does not have a major effect on the amount of blood cholesterol in most people, but it is best not to eat large quantities of these foods too often.

Fresh approach: when you are shopping for low fat foods, choose fresh seasonal vegetables (top right) and cook them without added fat. Salads (right) are a good accompaniment too, just use a polyunsaturated or monounsaturated oil for the dressing. Fresh fruits (above) are the perfect ending to a low fat meal if you haven't time to cook – eat them either raw in a salad or poach in fruit juice and serve hot with yogurt.

EASY WAYS TO CUT DOWN FAT AND SATURATED FAT

EAT LESS	TRY INSTEAD
Butter and hard fats.	Try spreading butter more thinly, or replace it with a low fat spread or polyunsaturated margarine.
Fatty meats and high fat products such as pies and sausages.	Buy the leanest cuts of meat you can afford and choose low fat meats like skinless chicken or turkey. Look for reduced-fat sausages and meat products. Eat fish more often, especially oily fish.
Full fat dairy products like cream, butter, hard margarine, milk and hard cheeses.	Choose skimmed or semi-skimmed milk and milk products, and try low fat yogurt, low fat fromage frais and lower fat cheeses such as skimmed milk soft cheese, reduced fat Cheddar, mozzarella or Brie.
Hard cooking fats such as lard or hard margarine.	Choose polyunsaturated oils for cooking, such as olive, sunflower, corn or soya oil.
Rich salad dressings like mayonnaise or salad cream.	Make salad dressings with low fat yogurt or fromage frais, or use a healthy oil such as olive oil.
Fried foods.	Grill, microwave, steam or bake when possible. Roast meats on a rack. Fill up on starchy foods like pasta, rice and couscous. Choose jacket or boiled potatoes, not chips.
Added fat in cooking.	Use heavy-based or non-stick pans so you can cook with little or no added fat.
High fat snacks such as crisps, chocolate, cakes, pastries and biscuits.	Choose fresh or dried fruit, breadsticks or vegetable sticks. Make your own low fat cakes and bakes.

STARTERS AND SNACKS

For a healthy diet it makes good sense to include some home-made soups in everyday meals, packed with the goodness of fresh ingredients and very low in fat. As a light lunch with crusty bread, or as a starter, modern soups are extremely quick and easy to make. The Thai-style Sweetcorn Soup takes only two to three minutes. An added bonus is the variety of fresh, seasonal vegetables available all year. Other starters can double up as a light dish or snack. It pays to have a selection of these healthy, quick snack foods handy. For simple snacks or packed lunches, pittas, Granary rolls or tacos can contain a tasty, low fat filling like chilli-spiced tuna salad. Some snacks are elegant enough for dinner party starters too.

CAULIFLOWER AND WALNUT CREAM

Even though there's no cream added to this soup, the cauliflower gives it a delicious, rich, creamy texture.

INGREDIENTS

Serves 4

1 medium cauliflower
1 medium onion, roughly chopped
450ml/¾ pint/1⅞ cups chicken or
   vegetable stock
450ml/¾ pint/1⅞ cups skimmed milk
45ml/3 tbsp walnut pieces
salt and black pepper
paprika and chopped walnuts, to
   garnish

1 Trim the cauliflower of outer leaves and break into small florets. Place the cauliflower, onion and stock in a large saucepan.

2 Bring to the boil, cover and simmer for about 15 minutes, or until soft. Add the milk and walnuts, then purée in a food processor until smooth.

3 Season the soup to taste, then bring to the boil. Serve sprinkled with paprika and chopped walnuts.

NUTRITION NOTES

Per portion:

Energy	166Kcals/699kJ
Fat	9.02g
Saturated fat	0.88g
Cholesterol	2.25mg
Fibre	2.73g

CURRIED CARROT AND APPLE SOUP

INGREDIENTS

Serves 4

10ml/2 tsp sunflower oil
15ml/1 tbsp mild Korma curry powder
500g/1¼ lb carrots, chopped
1 large onion, chopped
1 Bramley cooking apple, chopped
750ml/1¼ pints/3⅔ cups chicken stock
salt and black pepper
natural low fat yogurt and carrot curls,
   to garnish

NUTRITION NOTES

Per portion:

Energy	114Kcals/477kJ
Fat	3.57g
Saturated fat	0.43g
Cholesterol	0.4mg
Fibre	4.99g

1 Heat the oil and gently fry the curry powder for 2–3 minutes.

2 Add the carrots, onion and apple, stir well, then cover the pan.

3 Cook over a very low heat for about 15 minutes, shaking the pan occasionally until softened. Spoon the vegetable mixture into a food processor or blender, then add half the stock and process until smooth.

4 Return to the pan and pour in the remaining stock. Bring the soup to the boil and adjust the seasoning before serving in bowls, garnished with a swirl of yogurt and a few curls of carrot.

SPLIT PEA AND COURGETTE SOUP

Rich and satisfying, this tasty
and nutritious soup will warm a
chilly winter's day.

INGREDIENTS

Serves 4

175g/6oz/1⅞ cups yellow split peas
1 medium onion, finely chopped
5ml/1 tsp sunflower oil
2 medium courgettes, finely diced
900ml/1½ pints/3¾ cups chicken stock
2.5ml/½ tsp ground turmeric
salt and black pepper

1 Place the split peas in a bowl, cover
with cold water and leave to soak
for several hours or overnight. Drain,
rinse in cold water and drain again.

2 Cook the onion in the oil in a
covered pan, shaking occasionally,
until soft. Reserve a handful of diced
courgettes and add the rest to the pan.
Cook, stirring, for 2–3 minutes.

3 Add the stock and turmeric to the
pan and bring to the boil. Reduce
the heat, then cover and simmer for
30–40 minutes, or until the split peas
are tender. Adjust the seasoning.

4 When the soup is almost ready,
bring a large saucepan of water to
the boil, add the reserved diced courgettes and cook for 1 minute, then
drain and add to the soup before
serving hot with warm crusty bread.

COOK'S TIP
For a quicker alternative, use
split red lentils for this soup –
they need no presoaking and
cook very quickly. Adjust the
amount of stock, if necessary.

NUTRITION NOTES

Per portion:
Energy	174Kcals/730kJ
Fat	2.14g
Saturated fat	0.54g
Cholesterol	0
Fibre	3.43g

RED PEPPER SOUP WITH LIME

The beautiful rich red colour of this soup makes it a very attractive starter or light lunch. For a special dinner, toast some tiny croutons and serve sprinkled into the soup.

INGREDIENTS

Serves 4–6
4 red peppers, seeded and chopped
1 large onion, chopped
5ml/1 tsp olive oil
1 garlic clove, crushed
1 small red chilli, sliced
45ml/3 tbsp tomato purée
900ml/1½ pints/3¾ cups chicken stock
finely grated rind and juice of 1 lime
salt and black pepper
shreds of lime rind, to garnish

1 Cook the onion and peppers gently in the oil in a covered saucepan for about 5 minutes, shaking the pan occasionally, until softened.

2 Stir in the garlic, then add the chilli with the tomato purée. Stir in half the stock, then bring to the boil. Cover the pan and simmer for 10 minutes.

3 Cool slightly, then purée in a food processor or blender. Return to the pan, then add the remaining stock, the lime rind and juice, and seasoning.

4 Bring the soup back to the boil, then serve at once with a few strips of lime rind, scattered into each bowl.

NUTRITION NOTES	
Per portion:	
Energy	87Kcals/366kJ
Fat	1.57g
Saturated fat	0.12g
Cholesterol	0
Fibre	3.40g

BEETROOT AND APRICOT SWIRL

This soup is most attractive if you swirl together the two coloured mixtures, but if you prefer they can be mixed together to save on time and washing up.

INGREDIENTS

Serves 4
4 large cooked beetroot, roughly chopped
1 small onion, roughly chopped
600ml/1 pint/2½ cups chicken stock
200g/7oz/1 cup ready-to-eat dried apricots
250ml/8 fl oz/1 cup orange juice
salt and black pepper

1 Place the beetroot and half the onion in a pan with the stock. Bring to the boil, then reduce the heat, cover and simmer for about 10 minutes. Purée in a food processor or blender.

2 Place the rest of the onion in a pan with the apricots and orange juice, cover and simmer gently for about 15 minutes, until tender. Purée in a food processor or blender.

3 Return the two mixtures to the saucepans and reheat. Season to taste with salt and pepper, then swirl them together in individual soup bowls for a marbled effect.

COOK'S TIP
The apricot mixture should be the same consistency as the beetroot mixture – if it is too thick, then add a little more orange juice.

NUTRITION NOTES

Per portion:	
Energy	135Kcals/569kJ
Fat	0.51g
Saturated fat	0.01g
Cholesterol	0
Fibre	4.43g

THAI-STYLE SWEETCORN SOUP

This is a very quick and easy soup, made in minutes. If you are using frozen prawns, then defrost them first before adding to the soup.

INGREDIENTS

Serves 4

2.5ml/½ tsp sesame or sunflower oil
2 spring onions, thinly sliced
1 garlic clove, crushed
600ml/1 pint/2½ cups chicken stock
425g/15oz can cream-style sweetcorn
225g/8oz/1¼ cups cooked, peeled prawns
5ml/1 tsp green chilli paste or chilli sauce (optional)
salt and black pepper
fresh coriander leaves, to garnish

1 Heat the oil in a large heavy-based saucepan and sauté the onions and garlic over a medium heat for 1 minute, until softened, but not browned.

2 Stir in the chicken stock, cream-style sweetcorn, prawns and chilli paste or sauce, if using.

3 Bring the soup to the boil, stirring occasionally. Season to taste, then serve at once, sprinkled with fresh coriander leaves to garnish.

COOK'S TIP
If cream-style corn is not available, use ordinary canned sweetcorn, puréed in a food processor for a few seconds, until creamy yet with some texture left.

NUTRITION NOTES

Per portion:
Energy	202Kcals/848kJ
Fat	3.01g
Saturated fat	0.43g
Cholesterol	45.56mg
Fibre	1.6g

MEDITERRANEAN TOMATO SOUP

Children will love this soup –
especially if you use fancy shapes
of pasta such as alphabet or
animal shapes.

INGREDIENTS

Serves 4
675g/1½ lb ripe plum tomatoes
1 medium onion, quartered
1 celery stick
1 garlic clove
15ml/1 tbsp olive oil
450ml/¾ pint/1⅞ cups chicken stock
15ml/2 tbsp tomato purée
50g/2oz/½ cup small pasta shapes
salt and black pepper
fresh coriander or parsley, to garnish

1 Place the tomatoes, onion, celery
and garlic in a pan with the oil.
Cover and cook over a low heat for
40–45 minutes, shaking the pan
occasionally, until very soft.

2 Spoon the vegetables into a food
processor or blender and process
until smooth. Press though a sieve, then
return to the pan.

3 Stir in the stock and tomato purée
and bring to the boil. Add the pasta
and simmer gently for about 8 minutes,
or until the pasta is tender. Add salt
and pepper, to taste, then sprinkle with
coriander or parsley and serve hot.

NUTRITION NOTES

Per portion:

Energy	112Kcals/474kJ
Fat	3.61g
Saturated fat	0.49g
Cholesterol	0
Fibre	2.68g

MUSHROOM, CELERY AND GARLIC SOUP

INGREDIENTS

Serves 4
350g/12oz/3 cups chopped mushrooms
4 celery sticks, chopped
3 garlic cloves
45ml/3 tbsp dry sherry or white wine
750ml/1¼ pints/3⅔cups chicken stock
30ml/2 tbsp Worcestershire sauce
5ml/1 tsp grated nutmeg
salt and black pepper
celery leaves, to garnish

NUTRITION NOTES

Per portion:

Energy	48Kcals/200kJ
Fat	1.09g
Saturated fat	0.11g
Cholesterol	0
Fibre	1.64g

1 Place the mushrooms, celery and
garlic in a pan and stir in the sherry
or wine. Cover and cook over a low
heat for 30–40 minutes, until tender.

2 Add half the stock and purée in a
food processor or blender until
smooth. Return to the pan and add the
remaining stock, the Worcestershire
sauce and nutmeg.

3 Bring to the boil, season and serve
hot, garnished with celery leaves.

TOMATO AND CORIANDER SOUP

This delicious soup is an ideal solution when time is short but you still want to produce a very stylish starter.

INGREDIENTS

Serves 4

675g/1½lb small fresh tomatoes
30ml/2 tbsp vegetable oil
1 bay leaf
4 spring onions, cut into 2.5cm/1in
  pieces
5ml/1 tsp salt
5ml/1 tsp garlic pulp
5ml/1 tsp crushed black
  peppercorns
30ml/2 tbsp chopped fresh
  coriander
750ml/1¼ pints/3 cups water
15ml/1 tbsp cornflour
60ml/4 tbsp single cream, to garnish

1 To skin the tomatoes, plunge them into very hot water for 30 seconds, then transfer to a bowl of cold water. The skin should now peel off quickly and easily. Chop the tomatoes into large chunks.

2 Heat the oil in a large saucepan, add the bay leaf and spring onions, then stir in the tomatoes. Cook, stirring, for a few minutes more until the tomatoes are softened.

3 Add the salt, garlic, peppercorns, coriander and water, bring to the boil, then simmer for 15 minutes.

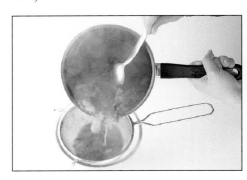

4 Dissolve the cornflour in a little water. Remove the soup from the heat and press through a sieve.

5 Return the soup to the pan, add the cornflour mixture and stir over a gentle heat until boiling and thickened.

6 Ladle the soup into shallow soup plates, then swirl a tablespoon of cream into each bowl before serving.

NUTRITION NOTES	
Per portion:	
Energy	113Kcals/474kJ
Fat	7.16g
Saturated fat	1.37g
Cholesterol	2.8mg

BUCKWHEAT BLINIS

Serves 4

5ml/1 tsp easy-blend dried yeast
250ml/8fl oz/1 cup skimmed milk,
   warmed
40g/1½oz/⅓ cup buckwheat flour
40g/1½oz/⅓ cup plain flour
10ml/2 tsp caster sugar
pinch of salt
1 egg, separated
lamb's lettuce, to serve

For the avocado cream

1 large avocado
75g/3oz/⅓ cup low fat fromage blanc
juice of 1 lime
cracked black peppercorns, to garnish

For the pickled beetroot

225g/8oz beetroot, peeled
45ml/3 tbsp lime juice
snipped fresh chives, to garnish

1 Mix the dried yeast with the milk, then mix with the next 4 ingredients and the egg yolk. Cover with a dish towel and leave to prove for about 40 minutes. Then whisk the egg white until stiff but not dry and fold into the blini mixture.

2 Heat a little oil in a non-stick frying pan and add a ladleful of batter to make a 10cm/4 in pancake. Cook for about 2–3 minutes on each side. Repeat with the remaining batter mixture to make eight blinis.

3 For the avocado cream, cut the avocado in half and remove the stone. Peel and place the flesh in a food processor or blender with the fromage blanc and lime juice. Process until the mixture is very smooth.

4 For the pickle, shred the beetroot finely. Mix with the lime juice. To serve, top each blini with a spoonful of avocado cream, garnish with cracked peppercorns. Serve with lamb's lettuce and the pickled beetroot, garnished with chives.

NUTRITION NOTES

Per portion:	
Energy	304Kcals/1277kJ
Fat	16.56g
Saturated fat	2.23g
Cholesterol	56.3mg
Fibre	3.3g

COOK'S TIP
Serve with a glass of chilled vodka for a special occasion.

AUBERGINE, GARLIC AND PEPPER PÂTÉ

Serve this chunky, garlicky pâté of smoky baked aubergine and red peppers on a bed of salad, accompanied by crispbreads.

INGREDIENTS

Serves 4

3 aubergines
2 red peppers
5 garlic cloves
7.5ml/1½ tsp pink peppercorns in brine, drained and crushed
30ml/2 tbsp chopped fresh coriander

NUTRITION NOTES

Per portion:	
Energy	70Kcals/292kJ
Fat	1.32g
Saturated fat	0
Cholesterol	0
Fibre	5.96g

1 Preheat the oven to 200°C/400°F/ Gas 6. Arrange the whole aubergines, peppers and garlic cloves on a baking sheet and place in the oven. After 10 minutes remove the garlic cloves, and turn over the aubergines and peppers.

2 Carefully peel the garlic cloves and place in the bowl of a food processor or blender.

3 After a further 20 minutes remove the blistered and charred peppers from the oven and place in a plastic bag. Leave to cool.

4 After a further 10 minutes remove the aubergines from the oven. Split in half and scoop the flesh into a sieve placed over a bowl. Press the flesh with a spoon to remove the bitter juices.

5 Add the aubergine flesh to the garlic in the food processor or blender, and process until smooth. Place in a large mixing bowl.

6 Peel and chop the red peppers and stir into the aubergine mixture. Mix in the peppercorns and fresh coriander, and serve at once.

CUCUMBER AND ALFALFA TORTILLAS

Wheat tortillas are extremely simple to prepare at home. Served with a crisp, fresh salsa, they make a marvellous starter, light lunch or supper dish.

INGREDIENTS

Serves 4

225g/8oz/2 cups plain flour, sifted
pinch of salt
45ml/3 tbsp olive oil
100–150ml/4–5fl oz/½–⅔ cup warm
    water
lime wedges, to garnish

For the salsa

1 red onion, finely chopped
1 red chilli, seeded and finely chopped
30ml/2 tbsp chopped fresh dill or
    coriander
½ cucumber, peeled and chopped
175g/6oz/2 cups alfalfa sprouts

For the sauce

1 large ripe avocado, peeled and stoned
juice of 1 lime
15ml/2 tbsp soft goat's cheese
pinch of paprika

1 Mix all the salsa ingredients together in a bowl and set aside.

2 For the sauce, place the avocado, lime juice and goat's cheese in a food processor or blender and process until smooth. Place in a bowl and cover with clear film. Dust with paprika just before serving.

3 For the tortillas, place the flour and salt in a food processor or blender, add the oil and process. Gradually add the water until a stiff dough has formed. Turn out on to a floured board and knead until smooth.

4 Divide the mixture into eight pieces. Knead each piece for a couple of minutes and form into a ball. Flatten and roll out each ball to a 23cm/9 in circle.

5 Heat a non-stick or ungreased heavy-based pan. Cook one tortilla at a time for about 30 seconds on each side. Place the cooked tortillas in a clean dish towel and repeat until you have made eight tortillas.

6 Spread each tortilla with a spoonful of avocado sauce, top with the salsa and roll up. Serve garnished with lime wedges and eat immediately.

NUTRITION NOTES	
Per portion:	
Energy	395Kcals/1659kJ
Fat	20.17g
Saturated fat	1.69g
Cholesterol	4.38mg
Fibre	4.15g

COOK'S TIP
When peeling the avocado be sure to scrape off the bright green flesh from immediately under the skin as this gives the sauce its vivid green colour.

CHEESE AND SPINACH PUFFS

INGREDIENTS

Serves 6

150g/5oz cooked, chopped spinach
175g/6oz/¾ cup cottage cheese
5ml/1 tsp grated nutmeg
2 egg whites
30ml/2 tbsp grated Parmesan cheese
salt and black pepper

1 Preheat the oven to 220°C/425°F/ Gas 7. Oil six ramekin dishes.

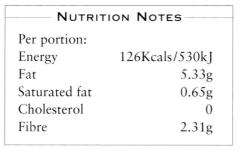

2 Mix together the spinach and cottage cheese in a small bowl, then add the nutmeg and seasoning to taste.

3 Whisk the egg whites in a separate bowl until stiff enough to hold soft peaks. Fold them evenly into the spinach mixture using a spatula or large metal spoon, then spoon the mixture into the oiled ramekins, dividing it evenly, and smooth the tops.

4 Sprinkle with the Parmesan and place on a baking sheet. Bake for 15–20 minutes, or until well risen and golden brown. Serve immediately.

NUTRITION NOTES

Per portion:

Energy	47Kcals/195kJ
Fat	1.32g
Saturated fat	0.52g
Cholesterol	2.79mg
Fibre	0.53g

LEMONY STUFFED COURGETTES

INGREDIENTS

Serves 4

4 courgettes, about 175g/6oz each
5ml/1 tsp sunflower oil
1 garlic clove, crushed
5ml/1 tsp ground lemon grass
finely grated rind and juice of ½ lemon
115g/4oz/1½ cups cooked long grain
  rice
175g/6oz cherry tomatoes, halved
30ml/2 tbsp toasted cashew nuts
salt and black pepper
sprigs of thyme, to garnish

NUTRITION NOTES

Per portion:

Energy	126Kcals/530kJ
Fat	5.33g
Saturated fat	0.65g
Cholesterol	0
Fibre	2.31g

1 Preheat the oven to 200°C/400°F/ Gas 6. Halve the courgettes lengthways and use a teaspoon to scoop out the centres. Blanch the shells in boiling water for 1 minute, then drain well.

2 Chop the courgette flesh finely and place in a saucepan with the oil and garlic. Stir over a moderate heat until softened, but not browned.

3 Stir in the lemon grass, lemon rind and juice, rice, tomatoes and cashew nuts. Season well and spoon into the courgette shells. Place the shells in a baking tin and cover with foil.

4 Bake for 25–30 minutes or until the courgettes are tender, then serve hot, garnished with thyme sprigs.

CHINESE GARLIC MUSHROOMS

Tofu is high in protein and very low in fat, so it is a very useful food to keep handy for quick meals and snacks like this one.

INGREDIENTS

Serves 4

8 large open mushrooms
3 spring onions, sliced
1 garlic clove, crushed
30ml/2 tbsp oyster sauce
285g/10 oz packet marinated tofu, cut
 into small dice
200g/7oz can sweetcorn, drained
10ml/2 tsp sesame oil
salt and black pepper

1 Preheat the oven to 200°C/400°F/ Gas 6. Finely chop the mushroom stalks and mix with the spring onions, garlic and oyster sauce.

2 Stir in the diced marinated tofu and sweetcorn, season well with salt and pepper, then spoon the filling into the mushrooms.

3 Brush the edges of the mushrooms with the sesame oil. Arrange the stuffed mushrooms in a baking dish and bake for 12–15 minutes, until the mushrooms are just tender, then serve at once.

COOK'S TIP
If you prefer, omit the oyster sauce and use light soy sauce instead.

NUTRITION NOTES

Per portion:

Energy	137Kcals/575kJ
Fat	5.6g
Saturated fat	0.85g
Cholesterol	0
Fibre	1.96g

SURPRISE SCOTCH 'EGGS'

This reduced fat version of
Scotch eggs is great for packed
lunches or picnics. If half fat
sausagemeat isn't available, buy
half fat sausages or turkey
sausages and remove the skins.

INGREDIENTS

Makes 3

*75ml/5 tbsp chopped parsley and
    snipped chives, mixed*
*115g/4oz/½ cup skimmed milk soft
    cheese*
450g/1 lb half fat sausagemeat
50g/2oz /½ cup rolled oats
salt and black pepper
mixed leaf and tomato salad, to serve

1 Preheat the oven to 200°C/400°F/
Gas 6. Mix together the herbs,
cheese and seasonings, then roll into
three even-sized balls.

2 Divide the sausagemeat into three
and press each piece out to a round,
about 1cm/½ in thick.

3 Wrap each cheese ball in a piece of
sausagemeat, smoothing over all the
joins to enclose the cheese completely.
Spread out the rolled oats on a plate
and roll the balls in the oats, using your
hands to coat them evenly.

4 Place the balls on a baking sheet
and bake for 30–35 minutes or
until golden. Serve hot or cold, with a
mixed leaf and tomato salad.

NUTRITION NOTES

Per portion:

Energy	352Kcals/1476kJ
Fat	15.94g
Saturated fat	0.29g
Cholesterol	66.38mg
Fibre	3.82g

CHICKEN NAAN POCKETS

INGREDIENTS

Serves 4

4 small naans
45ml/3 tbsp low fat natural yogurt
7.5ml/1½ tsp garam masala
5ml/1 tsp chilli powder
5ml/1 tsp salt
45ml/3 tbsp lemon juice
15ml/1 tbsp chopped fresh coriander
1 green chilli, chopped
450g/1 lb chicken without skin and
    bone, cubed
15ml/1 tbsp sunflower oil (optional)
8 onion rings
2 tomatoes, quartered
½ white cabbage, shredded

For the garnish
lemon wedges
2 small tomatoes, halved
mixed salad leaves
fresh coriander leaves

1 Cut into the middle of each naan to make a pocket, then set aside.

2 Mix together the yogurt, garam masala, chilli powder, salt, lemon juice, fresh coriander and chopped green chilli. Pour the marinade over the chopped chicken and leave to marinate for about 1 hour.

3 After 1 hour preheat the grill to very hot, then lower the heat to medium. Place the chicken in a flame-proof dish and grill for about 15–20 minutes until tender and cooked through, turning the chicken pieces at least twice. Baste with the oil while cooking if required.

COOK'S TIP
Use ready-made naans available in some supermarkets and Asian stores for speed.

4 Remove from the heat and fill each naan with the chicken and then with the onion rings, tomatoes and cabbage. Serve immediately with the garnish ingredients .

NUTRITION NOTES

Per portion:
Energy   364Kcals/1529kJ
Fat   10.85g
Saturated fat   3.01g
Cholesterol   65.64mg

CHICKEN TIKKA

INGREDIENTS

Serves 6

450g/1 lb chicken without skin and
    bone, chopped or cubed
5ml/1 tsp grated fresh root ginger
1 garlic clove, crushed
5ml/1 tsp chilli powder
1.5ml/¼ tsp turmeric
5ml/1 tsp salt
150ml/¼ pint/⅔ cup low fat
natural yogurt
60ml/4 tbsp lemon juice
15ml/1 tbsp chopped fresh coriander
15ml/1 tbsp sunflower oil

For the garnish
1 small onion, cut into rings
lime wedges
mixed salad
fresh coriander leaves

1 In a medium bowl, mix together the chicken pieces, ginger, garlic, chilli powder, turmeric, salt, yogurt, lemon juice and fresh coriander, and leave to marinate for at least 2 hours.

2 Place on a grill tray or in a flame-proof dish lined with foil and baste with the oil.

3 Preheat the grill to medium. Grill the chicken for about 15–20 minutes until cooked, turning and basting 2–3 times. Serve with the garnish ingredients.

COOK'S TIP
This is a quick and easy Indian starter. It can also be served as a main course for four.

NUTRITION NOTES

Per portion:
Energy   131Kcals/552kJ
Fat   5.5g
Saturated fat   1.47g
Cholesterol   44.07mg

TUNA CHILLI TACOS

Tacos are a useful, quick snack – but you will need to use both hands to eat them!

INGREDIENTS

Makes 8

8 taco shells
400g/14oz can red kidney beans, drained
120ml/4 fl oz/½ cup low fat fromage frais
2.5ml/½ tsp chilli sauce
2 spring onions, chopped
1 tsp/5 ml chopped fresh mint
½ small crisp lettuce, shredded
425g/15oz can tuna fish chunks in brine, drained
50g/2oz/¾ cup grated reduced fat Cheddar cheese
8 cherry tomatoes, quartered
mint sprigs, to garnish

1 Warm the taco shells in a hot oven for a few minutes until crisp.

2 Mash the beans lightly with a fork, then stir in the fromage frais with the chilli sauce, onions and mint.

3 Fill the taco shells with the shredded lettuce, the bean mixture and tuna. Top the filled shells with the cheese and serve at once with the tomatoes, garnished with sprigs of mint.

NUTRITION NOTES

Per portion:

Energy	147Kcals/615kJ
Fat	2.42g
Saturated fat	1.13g
Cholesterol	29.69mg
Fibre	2.41g

POTATO SKINS WITH CAJUN DIP

No need to deep fry potato skins for this treat – grilling crisps them up in no time.

INGREDIENTS

Serves 2

2 large baking potatoes
120g/4fl oz/½ cup natural yogurt
1 garlic clove, crushed
5ml/1 tsp tomato purée
2.5ml/½ tsp green chilli purée (or ½ small green chilli, chopped
1.25ml/¼ tsp celery salt
salt and black pepper

1 Bake or microwave the potatoes until tender. Cut them in half and scoop out the flesh, leaving a thin layer on the skins. Keep the scooped out potato for another meal.

2 Cut each potato in half again then place the pieces skin-side down on a large baking sheet.

3 Grill for 4–5 minutes, or until crisp. Mix together the dip ingredients and serve with the potato skins.

NUTRITION NOTES

Per portion:

Energy	202Kcals/847kJ
Fat	0.93g
Saturated fat	0.34g
Cholesterol	2.3mg
Fibre	3.03g

CHICKEN PITTAS WITH RED COLESLAW

Pittas are convenient for simple snacks and packed lunches and it's easy to pack in lots of fresh healthy ingredients.

INGREDIENTS

Serves 4

¼ red cabbage, finely shredded
1 small red onion, finely sliced
2 radishes, thinly sliced
1 red apple, peeled, cored and grated
15ml/1 tbsp lemon juice
45ml/3 tbsp low fat fromage frais
1 cooked chicken breast without skin,
  about 175g/6oz
4 large pittas or 8 small pittas
salt and black pepper
chopped fresh parsley, to garnish

1 Remove the tough central spine from the cabbage leaves, then finely shred the leaves using a large sharp knife. Place the shredded cabbage in a bowl and stir in the onion, radishes, apple and lemon juice.

2 Stir the fromage frais into the shredded cabbage mixture and season well with salt and pepper. Thinly slice the cooked chicken breast and stir into the shredded cabbage mixture until well coated in fromage frais.

3 Warm the pittas under a hot grill, then split them along one edge using a round-bladed knife. Spoon the filling into the pittas, then garnish with chopped fresh parsley.

> **COOK'S TIP**
> If the filled pittas need to be made more than an hour in advance, line the pitta breads with crisp lettuce leaves before adding the filling.

NUTRITION NOTES

Per portion:

Energy	232Kcals/976kJ
Fat	2.61g
Saturated fat	0.76g
Cholesterol	24.61mg
Fibre	2.97g

GRANARY SLTs

A quick, tasty snack or easy packed lunch with a healthy combination – sardines, lettuce and tomatoes!

INGREDIENTS

Serves 2

2 small Granary bread rolls
120g/4¼oz can sardines in olive oil
4 crisp green lettuce leaves, such as
 Webbs
1 beef tomato, sliced
Juice of ½ lemon
salt and black pepper

1 Slice the bread rolls in half crossways using a sharp knife. Drain off the oil from the sardines into a small bowl, then brush the cut surfaces of the rolls with a small amount of the oil.

2 Cut or break the sardines into small pieces, then fill each roll with a lettuce leaf, some sliced tomato and pieces of sardine, sprinkling the filling with a little lemon juice, and salt and pepper to taste.

3 Sandwich the rolls back together and press the lids down lightly with your hand. Serve at once.

NUTRITION NOTES

Per portion:

Energy	248Kcals/1042kJ
Fat	8.51g
Saturated fat	1.86g
Cholesterol	32.5mg
Fibre	3.01g

COOK'S TIP
If you prefer to use sardines in tomato sauce, spread the bread rolls thinly with low fat spread before adding the filling.

SPINACH AND POTATO GALETTE

Creamy layers of potato, spinach and herbs make this a warming supper dish.

INGREDIENTS

Serves 6

900g/2 lb large potatoes
450g/1 lb fresh spinach
2 eggs
400g/14oz/1¾ cups low fat soft cheese
15ml/1 tbsp wholegrain mustard
50g/2oz/2 cups chopped fresh herbs
   (e.g. chives, parsley, chervil or sorrel)
salt and black pepper
mixed salad, to serve

1 Preheat the oven to 180°C/350°F/ Gas 4. Line a deep 23cm/9 in cake tin with non-stick baking paper. Place the potatoes in a large saucepan and cover with cold water. Bring to the boil and cook for about 10 minutes. Drain well and allow to cool slightly before slicing thinly.

2 Wash the spinach and place in a large pan with only the water that is clinging to the leaves. Cover and cook, stirring once, until the spinach has just wilted. Drain well in a sieve and squeeze out the excess moisture. Chop finely.

NUTRITION NOTES	
Per portion:	
Energy	255Kcals/1072kJ
Fat	9.13g
Saturated fat	4.28g
Cholesterol	81.82mg
Fibre	3.81g

3 Beat the eggs with the soft cheese and mustard then stir in the chopped spinach and fresh herbs.

4 Place a layer of the sliced potatoes in the lined tin, arranging them in concentric circles. Top with a spoonful of the soft cheese mixture and spread out. Continue layering, seasoning with salt and pepper as you go, until all the potatoes and the soft cheese mixture are used up.

5 Cover the tin with a piece of foil and place in a roasting tin.

6 Fill the roasting tin with enough boiling water to come halfway up the sides, and cook in the oven for about 45–50 minutes. Serve hot or cold with a mixed salad.

SMOKED TROUT SALAD

Salads are the easy answer to fast, healthy eating. When lettuce is sweet and crisp, partner it with fillets of smoked trout, warm new potatoes and a creamy horseradish dressing.

INGREDIENTS

Serves 4
675g/1½ lb new potatoes
4 smoked trout fillets
115g/4oz mixed lettuce leaves
4 slices dark rye bread, cut into fingers
salt and black pepper

For the dressing
60ml/4 tbsp creamed horseradish
60ml/4 tbsp groundnut oil
15ml/1 tbsp white wine vinegar
10ml/2 tsp caraway seeds

NUTRITION NOTES

Per portion:
Energy	487Kcals/2044kJ
Fat	22.22g
Saturated fat	4.1g
Cholesterol	52.1mg
Fibre	3.5g

2 Remove the skin from the trout, then pull out any little bones using your fingers or a pair of tweezers.

4 Flake the trout fillets and halve the potatoes. Scatter them together with the rye fingers over the salad leaves and toss to mix. Season to taste and serve.

1 Peel or scrub the potatoes. Place the potatoes in a large saucepan and cover with cold water. Bring to the boil and simmer for about 20 minutes.

3 To make the dressing, place all the ingredients in a screw-top jar and shake vigorously. Season the lettuce leaves and moisten them with the prepared dressing. Divide the dressed leaves among four plates.

COOK'S TIP
To save time washing lettuce leaves, buy them ready-prepared from your supermarket. It is better to season the leaves rather than the dressing when making a salad.

SALMON PARCELS

Serve these little savoury parcels just as they are for a snack, or with a pool of fresh tomato sauce for a special starter.

INGREDIENTS

Makes 12
90g/3½oz can red or pink salmon
15ml/1 tbsp chopped fresh coriander
4 spring onions, finely chopped
4 sheets filo pastry
sunflower oil, for brushing
spring onions and salad leaves, to serve

> **COOK'S TIP**
> When you are using filo pastry, it is important to prevent it drying out; cover any you are not using with a tea towel or cling film.

1 Preheat the oven to 200°C/400°F/ Gas 6. Lightly oil a baking sheet. Drain the salmon, discarding any skin and bones, then place in a bowl.

2 Flake the salmon with a fork and mix with the fresh coriander and spring onions.

3 Place a single sheet of filo pastry on a work surface and brush lightly with oil. Place another sheet on top. Cut into six squares, about 10cm/4in. Repeat with the remaining pastry, to make 12 squares.

4 Place a spoonful of the salmon mixture on to each square. Brush the edges of the pastry with oil, then draw together, pressing to seal. Place the pastries on a baking sheet and bake for 12–15 minutes, until golden. Serve warm, with spring onions and salad.

NUTRITION NOTES	
Per portion:	
Energy	25Kcals/107kJ
Fat	1.16g
Saturated fat	0.23g
Cholesterol	2.55mg
Fibre	0.05g

TOMATO CHEESE TARTS

These crisp little tartlets are easier to make than they look. Best eaten fresh from the oven.

INGREDIENTS

Serves 4
2 sheets filo pastry
1 egg white
115g/4oz/½ cup skimmed milk soft cheese
handful fresh basil leaves
3 small tomatoes, sliced
salt and black pepper

1 Preheat the oven to 200°C/400°F/ Gas 6. Brush the sheets of filo pastry lightly with egg white and cut into sixteen 10 cm/4 in squares.

2 Layer the squares in twos, in eight patty tins. Spoon the cheese into the pastry cases. Season with black pepper and top with basil leaves.

3 Arrange tomatoes on the tarts, add seasoning and bake for 10-12 minutes, until golden. Serve warm.

NUTRITION NOTES	
Per portion:	
Energy	50Kcals/210kJ
Fat	0.33g
Saturated fat	0.05g
Cholesterol	0.29mg
Fibre	0.25g

MUSHROOM CROUSTADES

The rich mushroom flavour of this filling is heightened by the addition of Worcestershire sauce.

INGREDIENTS

Serves 2–4
1 short French stick, about 25cm/10in
10ml/2 tsp olive oil
250g/9oz open cup mushrooms, quartered
10ml/2 tsp Worcestershire sauce
10ml/2 tsp lemon juice
30ml/2 tbsp skimmed milk
30ml/2 tbsp snipped fresh chives
salt and black pepper
snipped fresh chives, to garnish

1 Preheat the oven to 200°C/400°F/ Gas 6. Cut the French bread in half lengthways. Cut a scoop out of the soft middle of each, leaving a thick border all the way round.

2 Brush the bread with oil, place on a baking sheet and bake for about 6–8 minutes, until golden and crisp.

3 Place the mushrooms in a small saucepan with the Worcestershire sauce, lemon juice and milk. Simmer for about 5 minutes, or until most of the liquid is evaporated.

4 Remove from the heat, then add the chives and seasoning. Spoon into the bread croustades and serve hot, garnished with snipped chives.

NUTRITION NOTES

Per portion:

Energy	324Kcals/1361kJ
Fat	6.4g
Saturated fat	1.27g
Cholesterol	0.3mg
Fibre	3.07g

TOMATO PESTO TOASTIES

Ready-made pesto is high in fat but, as its flavour is so powerful, it can be used in very small amounts with good effect, as in these tasty toasties.

INGREDIENTS

Serves 2
2 thick slices crusty bread
45ml/3 tbsp skimmed milk soft cheese
  or low fat fromage frais
10ml/2 tsp red or green pesto
1 beef tomato
1 red onion
salt and black pepper

1 Toast the bread slices on a hot grill until golden brown on both sides turning once. Leave to cool.

2 Mix together the skimmed milk soft cheese and pesto in a small bowl until well blended, then spread thickly on to the toasted bread.

3 Cut the beef tomato and red onion, crossways, into thin slices using a large sharp knife.

4 Arrange the slices, overlapping, on top of the toast and season with salt and pepper. Transfer the toasties to a grill rack and cook under a hot grill until heated through, then serve immediately.

> **COOK'S TIP**
> Almost any type of crusty bread can be used for this recipe, but Italian olive oil bread and French bread will give the best flavour.

NUTRITION NOTES	
Per portion:	
Energy	177Kcals/741kJ
Fat	2.41g
Saturated fat	0.19g
Cholesterol	0.23mg
Fibre	2.2g

SMOKED SALMON PANCAKES WITH PESTO

These simple pancakes are quick to prepare and are perfect for a special occasion topped with smoked salmon, fresh basil and toasted pine nuts.

INGREDIENTS

Makes 12–16
120ml/4fl oz/½ cup skimmed milk
115g/4oz/1 cup self-raising flour
1 egg
30ml/2 tbsp pesto sauce
vegetable oil, for frying
200ml/7fl oz/⅞ cup low fat crème fraîche
75g/3oz smoked salmon
15ml/1 tbsp pine nuts, toasted
salt and black pepper
12–16 basil sprigs, to garnish

NUTRITION NOTES

Per portion:
Energy	116Kcals/485kJ
Fat	7.42g
Saturated fat	2.4g
Cholesterol	39.58mg
Fibre	0.34g

1 Pour half of the milk into a mixing bowl. Add the flour, egg, pesto sauce and seasoning, and mix to a smooth batter.

2 Add the remainder of the milk and stir until evenly blended.

3 Heat the vegetable oil in a large frying pan. Spoon the pancake mixture into the heated oil in small heaps. Allow about 30 seconds for the pancakes to rise, then turn and cook briefly on the other side. Continue cooking the pancakes in batches until all the batter is used up.

4 Arrange the pancakes on a serving plate and top each one with a spoonful of crème fraîche.

5 Cut the salmon into 1cm/½ in strips and place on top of each pancake.

6 Scatter each pancake with pine nuts and garnish with a sprig of fresh basil before serving.

> COOK'S TIP
> If not serving immediately, cover the pancakes with a dish towel and keep warm in an oven pre-heated to 140°C/275°F/Gas 1.

WILD RICE RÖSTI WITH CARROT PURÉE

Rösti is a traditional dish from Switzerland. This variation has the extra nuttiness of wild rice and a bright simple sauce as a fresh accompaniment.

INGREDIENTS

Serves 6

50g/2oz/½ cup wild rice
900g/2 lb large potatoes
45ml/3 tbsp walnut oil
5ml/1 tsp yellow mustard seeds
1 onion, coarsely grated and drained
30ml/2 tbsp fresh thyme leaves
salt and black pepper
vegetables, to serve

For the purée

350g/12oz carrots, peeled and roughly
   chopped
pared rind and juice of 1 large orange

NUTRITION NOTES

Per portion:	
Energy	246Kcals/1035kJ
Fat	8.72g
Saturated fat	0.78g
Cholesterol	0
Fibre	3.8g

1 For the purée, place the carrots in a saucepan, cover with cold water and add two pieces of orange rind. Bring to the boil and cook for about 10 minutes or until tender. Drain well and discard the rind.

2 Purée the mixture in a food processor or blender with 60ml/4 tbsp of the orange juice. Return to the pan.

3 Place the wild rice in a clean pan and cover with water. Bring to the boil and cook for about 30–40 minutes, until the rice is just starting to split, but still crunchy. Drain the rice.

4 Scrub the potatoes, place in a large pan and cover with cold water. Bring to the boil and cook for about 10–15 minutes until just tender. Drain well and leave to cool slightly. When the potatoes are cool, peel and coarsely grate them into a large bowl. Add the cooked rice.

5 Heat 30ml/2 tbsp of the walnut oil in a non-stick frying pan and add the mustard seeds. When they start to pop, add the onion and cook gently for about 5 minutes until soft. Add to the bowl of potato and rice, together with the thyme, and mix thoroughly. Season.

6 Heat the remaining oil and add the potato mixture. Press down well and cook for about 10 minutes or until golden brown. Cover the pan with a plate and flip over, then slide the rösti back into the pan for another 10 minutes to cook the other side. Serve with the reheated carrot purée.

> COOK'S TIP
> Make individual rösti and serve topped with a mixed julienne of vegetables for an unusual starter.

AUBERGINE SUNFLOWER PÂTÉ

────── INGREDIENTS ──────

Serves 4
1 large aubergine
1 garlic clove, crushed
15ml/1 tbsp lemon juice
30ml/2 tbsp sunflower seeds
45ml/3 tbsp natural low fat yogurt
handful fresh coriander or parsley
black pepper
black olives, to garnish

1 Cut the aubergine in half and place, cut side down, on a baking sheet. Place under a hot grill for 15–20 minutes, until the skin is blackened and the flesh is soft. Leave for a few minutes, to cool slightly.

2 Scoop the flesh of the aubergine into a food processor. Add the garlic, lemon juice, sunflower seeds and yogurt. Process until smooth.

3 Roughly chop the fresh coriander or parsley and mix in. Season, then spoon into a serving dish. Top with olives and serve with vegetable sticks.

NUTRITION NOTES	
Per portion:	
Energy	71Kcals/298kJ
Fat	4.51g
Saturated fat	0.48g
Cholesterol	0.45mg
Fibre	2.62g

PEPPER DIPS WITH CRUDITÉS

Make one or both of these colourful vegetable dips – if you have time to make both they look spectacular together.

3 Stir half the breadcrumbs into each and season to taste with salt and pepper. Serve the dips with a selection of fresh vegetables for dipping.

────── INGREDIENTS ──────

Serves 4–6
2 medium red peppers, halved and
* seeded*
2 medium yellow peppers, halved and
* seeded*
2 garlic cloves
30ml/2 tbsp lemon juice
20ml/4 tsp olive oil
50g/2oz fresh white breadcrumbs
salt and black pepper
fresh vegetables, for dipping

2 Bring to the boil, then cover and simmer for 15 minutes until tender. Drain, cool, then purée separately in a food processor or blender, adding half the lemon juice and olive oil to each.

1 Place the peppers in separate saucepans with a peeled clove of garlic. Add just enough water to cover.

NUTRITION NOTES	
Per portion:	
Energy	103Kcals/432kJ
Fat	3.7g
Saturated fat	0.47g
Cholesterol	0
Fibre	2.77g

MEAT DISHES

There's no reason why meat should not be a valuable part of a low fat, low cholesterol diet, but you need to make careful choices when shopping, and adapt preparation and cooking methods to keep fats to a minimum. Remember that even lean meat has hidden fat, so grilling or roasting on a rack is an advantage, and any added fats should be low in saturates and used in moderation. A fat-trimmed roast needn't be dry, especially if you seal it with a moist, savoury crust as in Roast Pork in a Blanket. Even for casseroles, there's often no need to seal the meat in fat first – a non-stick pan will seal the meat in its own fat. Or choose stir-frying, which quickly seals the meat with just a touch of oil.

Good but meat too bland spice up with something

PORK AND CELERY POPOVERS

Lower in fat than they look, and a good way to make the meat go further, these little popovers will be popular with children.

INGREDIENTS

Serves 4
sunflower oil, for brushing
150g/5oz plain flour
1 egg white
250ml/8 fl oz/1 cup skimmed milk
120ml/4 fl oz/½ cup water
350g/12 oz lean minced pork
2 celery sticks, finely chopped
45ml/3 tbsp rolled oats
30ml/2 tbsp snipped chives
15ml/1 tbsp Worcestershire or brown sauce
salt and black pepper

1 Preheat the oven to 220°C/425°F/ Gas 7. Brush 12 deep patty tins with a very little oil.

2 Place the flour in a bowl and make a well in the centre. Add the egg white and milk and gradually beat in the flour. Gradually add the water, beating until smooth and bubbly.

3 Place the minced pork, celery, oats, chives, Worcestershire sauce and seasoning in a bowl and mix thoroughly. Mould the mixture into 12 small balls and place in the patty tins.

4 Cook for 10 minutes, remove from the oven and quickly pour the batter into the tins. Cook for a further 20–25 minutes, or until well risen and golden brown. Serve hot with thin gravy and fresh vegetables.

NUTRITION NOTES

Per portion:

Energy	344Kcals/1443kJ
Fat	9.09g
Saturated fat	2.7g
Cholesterol	61.62mg
Fibre	2.37g

BEEF AND MUSHROOM BURGERS

It's worth making your own burgers to cut down on fat – in these the meat is extended with mushrooms for extra fibre.

INGREDIENTS

Serves 4

1 small onion, chopped
150g/5oz/2 cups small cup mushrooms
450g/1 lb lean minced beef
50g/2oz/1 cup fresh wholemeal bread-
*   crumbs*
5ml/1 tsp dried mixed herbs
15ml/1 tbsp tomato purée
flour, for shaping
salt and black pepper

1 Place the onion and mushrooms in a food processor and process until finely chopped. Add the beef, bread-crumbs, herbs, tomato purée and seasonings. Process for a few seconds, until the mixture binds together but still has some texture.

2 Divide the mixture into 8–10 pieces, then press into burger shapes using lightly floured hands.

3 Cook the burgers in a non-stick frying pan, or under a hot grill for 12-15 minutes, turning once, until evenly cooked. Serve with relish and salad, in burger buns or pitta bread.

COOK'S TIP
The mixture is quite soft, so handle carefully and use a fish slice for turning to prevent the burgers from breaking up during cooking.

NUTRITION NOTES

Per portion	
Energy	196Kcals/822kJ
Fat	5.9g
Saturated fat	2.21g
Cholesterol	66.37mg
Fibre	1.60g

CURRIED LAMB AND LENTILS

This colourful curry is packed with protein and low in fat.

———— INGREDIENTS ————

Serves 4

8 lean, boneless lamb leg steaks, about
   500g/1¼ lb total weight
1 medium onion, chopped
2 medium carrots, diced
1 celery stick, chopped
15ml/1 tbsp hot curry paste
30ml/2 tbsp tomato purée
475ml/16 fl oz/2 cups stock
175g/6oz/1 cup green lentils
salt and black pepper
fresh coriander leaves, to garnish
boiled rice, to serve

1 In a large, non-stick pan, fry the lamb steaks without fat until browned, turning once.

2 Add the vegetables and cook for 2 minutes, then stir in the curry paste, tomato purée, stock and lentils.

3 Bring to the boil, cover and simmer gently for 30 minutes until tender. Add more stock, if necessary. Season and serve with coriander and rice.

NUTRITION NOTES

Per portion:

Energy	375Kcals/1575kJ
Fat	13.03g
Saturated fat	5.34g
Cholesterol	98.75mg
Fibre	6.11g

GOLDEN PORK AND APRICOT CASSEROLE

The rich golden colour and warm spicy flavour of this simple casserole make it ideal for chilly winter days.

———— INGREDIENTS ————

Serves 4

4 lean pork loin chops
1 medium onion, thinly sliced
2 yellow peppers, seeded and sliced
10ml/2 tsp medium curry powder
15ml/1 tbsp plain flour
250ml/8 fl oz/1 cup chicken stock
115g/4oz/⅔ cup dried apricots
30ml/2 tbsp wholegrain mustard
salt and black pepper

1 Trim the excess fat from the pork and fry without fat in a large, heavy or non-stick pan until lightly browned.

2 Add the onion and peppers to the pan and stir over a moderate heat for 5 minutes. Stir in the curry powder and the flour.

3 Add the stock, stirring, then add the apricots and mustard. Cover and simmer for 25–30 minutes, until tender. Adjust the seasoning and serve hot, with rice or new potatoes.

NUTRITION NOTES

Per portion:

Energy	289Kcals/1213kJ
Fat	10.03g
Saturated fat	3.23g
Cholesterol	82.8mg
Fibre	4.86g

COUNTRY PORK WITH PARSLEY COBBLER

This hearty casserole is a complete main course in one pot.

INGREDIENTS

Serves 4

450g/1 lb boneless pork shoulder, diced
1 small swede, diced
2 carrots, sliced
2 parsnips, sliced
2 leeks, sliced
2 celery sticks, sliced
750ml/1¼ pint/3⅔ cups boiling beef stock
30ml/2 tbsp tomato purée
30ml/2 tbsp chopped fresh parsley
50g/2oz/¼ cup pearl barley
celery salt and black pepper

For the topping

150g/5oz/1 cup plain flour
5ml/1 tsp baking powder
90ml/6 tbsp low fat fromage frais
45ml/3 tbsp chopped fresh parsley

1 Preheat the oven to 180°C/350°F/ Gas 4. Fry the pork without fat, in a non-stick pan until lightly browned.

2 Add the vegetables to the pan and stir over a medium heat until lightly coloured. Tip into a large casserole dish, then stir in the stock, tomato purée, parsley and pearl barley.

3 Season with celery salt and pepper, then cover and place in the oven for about 1–1¼ hours, until the pork and vegetables are tender.

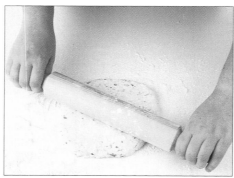

4 For the topping, sift the flour and baking powder with seasoning, then stir in the fromage frais and parsley with enough cold water to mix to a soft dough. Roll out to about 1cm/½ in thickness and cut into 12–16 triangles.

5 Remove the casserole from the oven and raise the temperature to 220°C/ 425°F/Gas 7.

6 Arrange the triangles over the casserole, overlapping. Bake for 15–20 minutes, until well risen and golden.

NUTRITION NOTES

Per portion:

Energy	461Kcals/1936kJ
Fat	10.55g
Saturated fat	3.02g
Cholesterol	77.85mg
Fibre	9.44g

BEEF STRIPS WITH ORANGE AND GINGER

Stir-frying is one of the best ways to cook with the minimum of fat. It's also one of the quickest ways to cook, but you do need to choose tender meat.

INGREDIENTS

Serves 4
450g/1 lb lean beef rump, fillet or sirloin,
  cut into thin strips
finely grated rind and juice of 1 orange
15ml/1 tbsp light soy sauce
5ml/1 tsp cornflour
2.5cm/1in piece root ginger, finely
  chopped
10ml/2 tsp sesame oil
1 large carrot, cut into thin strips
2 spring onions, thinly sliced

1 Place the beef strips in a bowl and sprinkle over the orange rind and juice. If possible, leave to marinate for at least 30 minutes.

2 Drain the liquid from the meat and set aside, then mix the meat with the soy sauce, cornflour and ginger.

4 Stir in the spring onions and reserved liquid, then cook, stirring, until boiling and thickened. Serve hot with rice noodles or plain boiled rice.

3 Heat the oil in a wok or large frying pan and add the beef. Stir-fry for 1 minute until lightly coloured, then add the carrot and stir-fry for a further 2–3 minutes.

NUTRITION NOTES

Per portion:

Energy	175Kcals/730kJ
Fat	6.81g
Saturated fat	2.31g
Cholesterol	66.37mg
Fibre	0.67g

GREEK LAMB PIE

INGREDIENTS

Serves 4

sunflower oil, for brushing
450g/1 lb lean minced lamb
1 medium onion, sliced
1 garlic clove, crushed
400g/14oz can plum tomatoes
30ml/2 tbsp chopped fresh mint
5ml/1 tsp grated nutmeg
350g/12oz young spinach leaves
270g/10 oz packet filo pastry
5ml/1 tsp sesame seeds
salt and black pepper

1 Preheat the oven to 200°C/400°F/ Gas 6. Lightly oil a 22cm/8½ in round spring form tin.

2 Fry the mince and onion without fat in a non-stick pan until golden. Add the garlic, tomatoes, mint, nutmeg and seasoning. Bring to the boil, stirring. Simmer, stirring occasionally, until most of the liquid has evaporated.

3 Wash the spinach and remove any tough stalks, then cook in only the water clinging to the leaves for about 2 minutes, until wilted.

4 Lightly brush each sheet of filo pastry with oil and lay in overlapping layers in the tin, leaving enough overhanging to wrap over the top.

5 Spoon in the meat and spinach, then wrap the pastry over to enclose, scrunching it slightly. Sprinkle with sesame seeds and bake for about 25–30 minutes, or until golden and crisp. Serve hot, with salad or vegetables.

NUTRITION NOTES

Per portion:

Energy	444Kcals/1865kJ
Fat	15.36g
Saturated fat	5.51g
Cholesterol	88.87mg
Fibre	3g

ROAST PORK IN A BLANKET

INGREDIENTS

Serves 4

1.5kg/3 lb lean pork loin joint
1 eating apple, cored and grated
40g/1½oz/¼ cup fresh breadcrumbs
30ml/2 tbsp chopped hazelnuts
15ml/1 tbsp Dijon mustard
15ml/1 tbsp snipped fresh chives
salt and black pepper

1 Cut the skin from the pork leaving a thin layer of fat.

2 Preheat the oven to 220°C/425°F/ Gas 7. Place the meat on a rack in a roasting tin, cover with foil and roast for 1 hour, then reduce the oven temperature to 180°C/350°F/Gas 4.

3 Mix together the apple, breadcrumbs, nuts, mustard, chives and seasoning. Remove the foil and spread the breadcrumb mixture over the fat surface of the meat.

4 Cook the pork for 45–60 minutes, or until the meat juices run clear. Serve in slices with a rich gravy.

NUTRITION NOTES

Per portion:

Energy	367Kcals/1540kJ
Fat	18.73g
Saturated fat	5.19g
Cholesterol	129.38mg
Fibre	1.5g

Stuffed Aubergines with Lamb

Ingredients

Serves 4

2 aubergines
30ml/2 tbsp sunflower oil
1 onion, sliced
5ml/1 tsp grated fresh root ginger
5ml/1 tsp chilli powder
1 garlic clove, crushed
1.5ml/¼ tsp turmeric
5ml/1 tsp salt
5ml/1 tsp ground coriander
1 tomato, chopped
350g/12oz lean leg of lamb, minced
1 green pepper, roughly chopped
1 orange pepper, roughly chopped
30ml/2 tbsp chopped fresh coriander

For the garnish

½ onion, sliced
2 cherry tomatoes, quartered
fresh coriander leaves

Nutrition Notes

Per portion:
Energy	239Kcals/1003kJ
Fat	13.92g
Saturated fat	4.36g
Cholesterol	67.15mg

1 Cut the aubergines in half lengthways and cut out most of the flesh and discard. Place the aubergine shells in a lightly greased ovenproof dish.

2 In a saucepan, heat 15ml/1 tbsp oil and fry the onion until golden. Gradually stir in the ginger, chilli powder, garlic, turmeric, salt and ground coriander. Add the tomato, lower the heat and stir-fry for 5 minutes.

3 Preheat the oven to 180°C/350°F/ Gas 4. Add the minced lamb and stir-fry over a medium heat for a further 7–10 minutes.

4 Add the chopped peppers and fresh coriander to the lamb mixture, and stir well.

5 Spoon the lamb mixture into the aubergine shells and brush the edges of the shells with the remaining oil. Bake in the preheated oven for about 20–25 minutes until cooked through and browned on top.

6 Serve with the garnish ingredients and either a green salad or plain boiled rice.

Cook's Tip

For a special occasion, stuffed baby aubergines look particularly attractive. Use four small aubergines, leaving the stalks intact, and prepare and cook as described above. Reduce the baking time slightly, if necessary. Large tomatoes or courgettes also make a good alternative to aubergines.

BEEF WITH GREEN BEANS

This easy-to-cook curried dish is a delicious variation on a traditional Indian recipe.

INGREDIENTS

Serves 4

275g/10oz fine green beans, cut into
  2.5cm/1 in pieces
30ml/2 tbsp sunflower oil
1 medium onion, sliced
5ml/1 tsp grated fresh root ginger
1 garlic clove, crushed
5ml/1 tsp chilli powder
6.5ml/1¼ tsp salt
1.5ml/¼ tsp turmeric
2 tomatoes, chopped
450g/1 lb lean beef, cubed
1.2 litres/2 pints/5 cups water
15ml/1 tbsp chopped fresh coriander
1 red pepper, sliced
2 green chillies, chopped

1 Cook the green beans in a saucepan of boiling salted water for about 5 minutes, then drain and set aside.

2 Heat the oil in a large saucepan and fry the sliced onion until golden.

3 Mix together the ginger, garlic, chilli powder, salt, turmeric and chopped tomatoes. Spoon into the onions and stir-fry for about 5–7 minutes.

4 Add the beef and stir-fry for a further 3 minutes. Pour in the water, bring to the boil and lower the heat. Cover and cook for about 45–60 minutes until most of the water has evaporated and the meat is tender.

5 Add the green beans and mix everything together well.

6 Finally, add the red pepper, fresh coriander and chopped green chillies and cook for a further 7–10 minutes stirring occasionally. Serve hot with wholemeal chapatis.

NUTRITION NOTES

Per portion:

Energy	241Kcals/1012kJ
Fat	11.6g
Saturated fat	2.89g
Cholesterol	66.96mg

MEXICAN BEEF BURGERS

Nothing beats the flavour and quality of a home-made burger. This version is from Mexico and is delicately seasoned with cumin and fresh coriander.

INGREDIENTS

Makes 4

4 corn on the cob
50g/2oz/1 cup stale white breadcrumbs
90ml/6 tbsp skimmed milk
1 small onion, finely chopped
5ml/1 tsp ground cumin
2.5ml/½ tsp cayenne pepper
2.5ml/½ tsp celery salt
45ml/3 tbsp chopped fresh coriander
900g/2 lb lean minced beef
4 sesame buns
60ml/4 tbsp reduced calorie mayonnaise
4 tomato slices
½ iceberg lettuce or other leaves such as frisée or Webb's
salt and black pepper
1 large packet corn chips, to serve

1 Cook the corn cobs in a large saucepan of boiling water for about 15 minutes.

2 Combine the breadcrumbs, skimmed milk, onion, cumin, cayenne, celery salt and fresh coriander together in a large bowl.

3 Add the beef and mix by hand until the mixture is evenly blended.

4 Divide the beef mixture into four portions and flatten between sheets of clear film.

5 Preheat a moderate grill and cook for about 10 minutes for medium or 15 minutes for well-done burgers.

6 Split and toast the buns, spread with mayonnaise and sandwich the burgers with the tomato slices, lettuce leaves and seasoning. Serve with corn chips and the corn on the cob.

NUTRITION NOTES	
Per portion:	
Energy	563Kcals/2363kJ
Fat	18.82g
Saturated fat	5.55g
Cholesterol	133.2mg

PORK STEAKS WITH GREMOLATA

Gremolata is a popular Italian dressing of garlic, lemon and parsley – it adds a hint of sharpness to the pork.

INGREDIENTS

Serves 4
30ml/2 tbsp olive oil
4 lean pork shoulder steaks, about
   175g/6oz each
1 onion, chopped
2 garlic cloves, crushed
30ml/2 tbsp tomato purée
400g/14oz can chopped tomatoes
150ml/¼ pint/⅔ cup dry white wine
bouquet garni
3 anchovy fillets, drained and chopped
salt and black pepper
salad leaves, to serve

For the gremolata
45ml/3 tbsp chopped fresh parsley
grated rind of ½ lemon
grated rind of 1 lime
1 garlic clove, chopped

1 Heat the oil in a large flameproof casserole, add the pork steaks and brown on both sides. Remove the steaks from the casserole.

2 Add the onion to the casserole and cook until soft and beginning to brown. Add the garlic and cook for about 1–2 minutes, then stir in the tomato purée, chopped tomatoes and wine. Add the bouquet garni. Bring to the boil, then boil rapidly for a further 3–4 minutes to reduce the sauce and thicken slightly.

3 Return the pork to the casserole, then cover and cook for about 30 minutes. Stir in the anchovies.

4 Cover the casserole and cook for a further 15 minutes, or until the pork is tender. For the gremolata, mix together the parsley, lemon and lime rinds and garlic.

5 Remove the pork steaks and discard the bouquet garni. Reduce the sauce over a high heat, if it is not already thick. Taste and adjust the seasoning if required.

6 Return the pork to the casserole, then sprinkle with the gremolata. Cover and cook for a further 5 minutes, then serve hot with salad leaves.

NUTRITION NOTES	
Per portion:	
Energy	267Kcals/1121kJ
Fat	13.39g
Saturated fat	3.43g
Cholesterol	69mg
Fibre	2.06g

PAN-FRIED MEDITERRANEAN LAMB

The warm summery flavours of the Mediterranean are combined for a simple weekday meal.

INGREDIENTS

Serves 4

8 lean lamb cutlets
1 medium onion, thinly sliced
2 red peppers, seeded and sliced
400g/14oz can plum tomatoes
1 garlic clove, crushed
45ml/3 tbsp chopped fresh basil leaves
30ml/2 tbsp chopped black olives
salt and black pepper

1 Trim any excess fat from the lamb, then fry without fat in a non-stick pan until golden brown.

2 Add the onion and peppers to the pan. Cook, stirring, for a few minutes to soften, then add the plum tomatoes, garlic and basil.

3 Cover and simmer for 20 minutes or until the lamb is tender. Stir in the olives, season and serve hot with pasta.

NUTRITION NOTES

Per portion:

Energy	224Kcals/939kJ
Fat	10.17g
Saturated fat	4.32g
Cholesterol	79mg
Fibre	2.48g

BACON KOFTAS

These easy koftas are good for barbecues and summer grills, served with lots of salad.

INGREDIENTS

Serves 4

225g/8oz lean smoked back bacon,
    roughly chopped
75g/3oz/1½ cups fresh wholemeal
    breadcrumbs
2 spring onions, chopped
15ml/1 tbsp chopped fresh parsley
finely grated rind of 1 lemon
1 egg white
black pepper
paprika
lemon rind and fresh parsley leaves, to
    garnish

1 Place the bacon in a food processor with the breadcrumbs, spring onions, parsley, lemon rind, egg white and pepper. Process the mixture until it is finely chopped and begins to bind together. Alternatively, use a mincer.

2 Divide the bacon mixture into eight even-sized pieces and shape into long ovals around eight wooden or bamboo skewers.

3 Sprinkle the koftas with paprika and cook under a hot grill or on a barbecue for about 8–10 minutes, turning occasionally, until browned and cooked through. Garnish with lemon rind and parsley leaves, then serve hot with lemon rice and salad.

NUTRITION NOTES

Per portion:

Energy	128Kcals/538kJ
Fat	4.7g
Saturated fat	1.61g
Cholesterol	10.13mg
Fibre	1.33g

SAUSAGE BEANPOT WITH DUMPLINGS

Sausages needn't be totally banned on a low fat diet, but choose them carefully. If you are unable to find a reduced-fat variety, choose turkey sausages instead, and always drain off any fat during cooking.

INGREDIENTS

Serves 4
450g/1 lb half-fat sausages
1 medium onion, thinly sliced
1 green pepper, seeded and diced
1 small red chilli, sliced, or 2.5ml/½ tsp chilli sauce
400g/14oz can chopped tomatoes
250ml/8 fl oz/1 cup beef stock
425g/15oz can red kidney beans, drained
salt and black pepper

For the dumplings
275g/10oz/2½ cups plain flour
10ml/2 tsp baking powder
225g/8oz/1 cup cottage cheese

1 Fry the sausages without fat in a non-stick pan until brown. Add the onion and pepper. Stir in the chilli, tomatoes and stock; bring to the boil.

NUTRITION NOTES

Per portion:
Energy	574Kcals/2409kJ
Fat	13.09g
Saturated fat	0.15g
Cholesterol	52.31mg
Fibre	9.59g

2 Cover and simmer gently for 15–20 minutes, then add the beans and bring to the boil.

3 To make the dumplings, sift the flour and baking powder together and add enough water to mix to a firm dough. Roll out thinly and stamp out 16–18 rounds using a 7.5cm/3in cutter.

4 Place a small spoonful of cottage cheese on each round and bring the edges of the dough together, pinching to enclose. Arrange the dumplings over the sausages in the pan, cover the pan and simmer for 10–12 minutes, until the dumplings are well risen. Serve hot.

SPICY SPRING LAMB ROAST

INGREDIENTS

Serves 6

1.5kg/3–3½ lb lean leg spring lamb
5ml/1 tsp chilli powder
1 garlic clove, crushed
5ml/1 tsp ground coriander
5ml/1 tsp ground cumin
5ml/1 tsp salt
10ml/2 tsp desiccated coconut
10ml/2 tsp ground almonds
45ml/3 tbsp low fat natural yogurt
30ml/2 tbsp lemon juice
30ml/2 tbsp sultanas
30ml/2 tbsp corn oil

For the garnish

mixed salad leaves
fresh coriander leaves
2 tomatoes, sliced
1 large carrot, cut into julienne strips
lemon wedges

NUTRITION NOTES

Per portion:

Energy	197Kcals/825kJ
Fat	11.96g
Saturated fat	4.7g
Cholesterol	67.38mg

1 Preheat the oven to 180°C/350°F/ Gas 4. Trim off the fat, rinse and pat dry the leg of lamb and set aside on a sheet of foil large enough to enclose the whole joint.

2 In a medium bowl, mix together the chilli powder, garlic, ground coriander, ground cumin and salt.

3 In a food processor or blender process together the desiccated coconut, ground almonds, yogurt, lemon juice and sultanas until you have a smooth texture.

4 Add the contents of the food processor to the spice mixture together with the corn oil and mix together. Pour this on to the leg of lamb and rub over the meat.

5 Enclose the meat in the foil and place in an ovenproof dish. Cook in the preheated oven for 1½ hours.

6 Remove the lamb from the oven, open the foil and, using the back of a spoon, spread the mixture evenly over the meat again. Return the lamb, uncovered, to the oven for a further 45 minutes or until it is cooked right through and tender. Slice the meat and serve with the garnish ingredients.

LAMB PIE WITH MUSTARD THATCH

A pleasant change from a classic shepherd's pie – healthier, too.

INGREDIENTS

Serves 4

750g/1½ lb old potatoes, diced
30ml/2 tbsp skimmed milk
15ml/1 tbsp wholegrain or French
    mustard
450g/1 lb lean minced lamb
1 onion, chopped
2 celery sticks, sliced
2 carrots, diced
150ml/¼ pint/⅔ cup beef stock
60ml/4 tbsp rolled oats
15ml/1 tbsp Worcestershire sauce
30ml/2 tbsp fresh chopped rosemary,
    or 10ml/2 tsp dried
salt and black pepper

1 Cook the potatoes in boiling, lightly salted water until tender. Drain and mash until smooth, then stir in the milk and mustard. Meanwhile, preheat the oven to 200°C/400°F/Gas 6.

2 Break up the lamb with a fork and fry without fat in a non-stick pan until lightly browned. Add the onion, celery and carrots to the pan and cook for 2–3 minutes, stirring.

3 Stir in the stock and rolled oats. Bring to the boil, then add the Worcestershire sauce and rosemary and season to taste with salt and pepper.

4 Turn the meat mixture into a 1.8 litre/3 pint/7 cup ovenproof dish and spread over the potato topping evenly, swirling with the edge of a knife. Bake for 30–35 minutes, or until golden. Serve hot with fresh vegetables.

NUTRITION NOTES	
Per portion:	
Energy	422Kcals/1770kJ
Fat	12.41g
Saturated fat	5.04g
Cholesterol	89.03mg
Fibre	5.07g

INDONESIAN PORK AND PEANUT SATÉ

These delicious skewers of pork are popular street food in Indonesia. They are quick to make and eat.

INGREDIENTS

Serves 4

400g/14oz/2 cups long grain rice
450g/1 lb lean pork
pinch of salt
2 limes, quartered, and a chilli, to garnish
115g/4oz green salad, to serve

For the sauce

15ml/1 tbsp sunflower oil
1 small onion, chopped
1 garlic clove, crushed
2.5ml/½ tsp hot chilli sauce
15ml/1 tbsp sugar
30ml/2 tbsp soy sauce
30ml/2 tbsp lemon or lime juice
2.5ml/½ tsp anchovy essence (optional)
60ml/4 tbsp smooth peanut butter

1 Place the rice in a large saucepan, and cover with 900ml/1½ pints/3¾ cups of boiling salted water, stir and simmer uncovered for about 15 minutes until the liquid has been absorbed. Switch off the heat, cover and stand for 5 minutes.

2 Slice the pork into thin strips, then thread zig-zag fashion on to sixteen bamboo skewers.

3 To make the sauce, very gently heat the sunflower oil in a pan. Add the onion and cook over a low heat to soften without colouring for about 3–4 minutes. Add the next five ingredients and the anchovy essence, if using. Simmer briefly, then gently stir in the peanut butter.

VARIATION
Indonesian saté can also be prepared with lean beef, chicken or prawns for a delicious alternative.

4 Arrange the skewers on a baking tray and spoon over a third of the sauce. Grill for 6–8 minutes, turning once. Serve on a bed of rice, accompanied by the remaining sauce. Garnish with the limes and chilli and serve with a salad.

NUTRITION NOTES

Per portion:	
Energy	689Kcals/2895kJ
Fat	21.07g
Saturated fat	4.95g
Cholesterol	77.62mg
Fibre	1.39g

RUBY BACON CHOPS

This sweet, tangy sauce works well with lean bacon chops.

INGREDIENTS

Serves 4
1 ruby grapefruit
4 lean bacon loin chops
45ml/3 tbsp redcurrant jelly
black pepper

NUTRITION NOTES

Per portion:

Energy	215Kcals/904kJ
Fat	8.40g
Saturated fat	3.02g
Cholesterol	20.25mg
Fibre	0.81g

1 Cut away all the peel and pith from the grapefruit, using a sharp knife, and carefully remove the segments, catching the juice in a bowl.

2 Fry the bacon chops in a non-stick frying pan without fat, turning them once, until golden and cooked.

3 Add the reserved grapefruit juice and redcurrant jelly to the pan and stir until melted. Add the grapefruit segments, then season with pepper and serve hot with fresh vegetables.

JAMAICAN BEANPOT

If pumpkin is not available, use any other type of squash, or try swede instead. This recipe is a good one to double – or even treble – for a crowd.

INGREDIENTS

Serves 4
450g/1 lb braising steak, diced
1 small pumpkin, about 450g/1 lb diced flesh
1 medium onion, chopped
1 green pepper, seeded and sliced
15ml/1 tbsp paprika
2 garlic cloves, crushed
2.5ml/1 in piece fresh ginger root, chopped
400g/14oz can chopped tomatoes
115g/4oz baby corn cobs
250ml/8 fl oz/1 cup beef stock
425g/15oz can chick-peas, drained
425g/15oz can red kidney beans, drained
salt and black pepper

1 Fry the diced beef without fat in a large flameproof casserole, stirring to seal it on all sides.

2 Stir in the pumpkin, onion and pepper, cook for a further 2 minutes, then add the paprika, garlic and ginger.

3 Stir in the tomatoes, corn and stock, then bring to the boil. Cover and simmer for 40–45 minutes or until tender. Add the chick-peas and beans and heat thoroughly. Adjust the seasoning with salt and pepper to taste and serve hot with couscous or rice.

NUTRITION NOTES

Per portion:

Energy	357Kcals/1500kJ
Fat	8.77g
Saturated fat	2.11g
Cholesterol	66.37mg
Fibre	10.63g

BUTTERFLIED CUMIN AND GARLIC LAMB

Ground cumin and garlic give the lamb a wonderful Middle Eastern flavour, although you may prefer a simple oil, lemon and herb marinade instead.

INGREDIENTS

Serves 6
1.75kg/4–4½ lb lean leg of lamb
60ml/4 tbsp olive oil
30ml/2 tbsp ground cumin
4–6 garlic cloves, crushed
salt and black pepper
coriander leaves and lemon wedges,
   to garnish
toasted almond and raisin-studded rice,
   to serve

1 To butterfly the lamb, cut away the meat from the bone using a small sharp knife. Remove any excess fat and the thin, parchment-like membrane. Bat out the meat to an even thickness, then prick the fleshy side of the lamb well with the tip of a knife.

2 In a bowl, mix together the oil, cumin and garlic, and season with pepper. Spoon the mixture all over the lamb, then rub it well into the crevices. Cover and leave to marinate overnight.

3 Preheat the oven to 200°C/400°F/ Gas 6. Spread the lamb, skin-side down, on a rack in a roasting tin. Season with salt, and roast for about 45–60 minutes, until crusty brown outside, pink in the centre.

4 Remove the lamb from the oven and leave it to rest for about 10 minutes. Cut into diagonal slices and serve with the toasted almond and raisin-studded rice. Garnish with coriander leaves and lemon wedges.

NUTRITION NOTES

Per portion:
Energy	387Kcals/1624kJ
Fat	24.42g
Saturated fat	8.72g
Cholesterol	144.83mg
Fibre	0.14g

COOK'S TIP
The lamb may be barbecued – thread it on to two long skewers and cook on a hot barbecue for 20–25 minutes on each side.

SKEWERS OF LAMB WITH MINT

A delicious way to serve lamb with a Mediterranean twist. This dish could also be cooked on a barbecue and eaten al fresco-style in the garden.

INGREDIENTS

Serves 4

300ml/½ pint/1¼ cups low fat natural yogurt
½ garlic clove, crushed
good pinch of saffron powder
30ml/2 tbsp chopped fresh mint
30ml/2 tbsp clear honey
45ml/3 tbsp olive oil
3 lean lamb neck fillets, about 675g/1½ lb
1 aubergine
2 small red onions, quartered
salt and black pepper
small mint leaves, to garnish
lettuce and hot pitta bread, to serve

COOK'S TIP
If using bamboo skewers, soak them in cold water before use to prevent them burning. All lean, not-too-thick cuts of meat such as lamb or chicken grill very well on a barbecue. Meat should be marinated beforehand and left overnight if at all possible.

1 In a shallow dish, mix together the yogurt, garlic, saffron, mint, honey, oil and ground black pepper.

2 Trim the lamb and cut into 2.5cm/1 in cubes. Add to the marinade and stir until well coated. Leave to marinate for at least 4 hours.

3 Cut the aubergine into 2.5cm/1 in cubes and blanch in boiling salted water for 1–2 minutes. Drain well.

4 Preheat the grill. Remove the lamb cubes from the marinade. Thread the lamb, aubergine and onion pieces alternately on to skewers. Grill for about 10–12 minutes, turning and basting occasionally with the marinade, until the lamb is tender. Serve the skewers on a bed of lettuce, garnished with mint leaves and accompanied by hot pitta bread.

NUTRITION NOTES	
Per portion:	
Energy	484Kcals/2032kJ
Fat	30.35g
Saturated fat	12.54g
Cholesterol	143.06mg
Fibre	2.05g

PAN-FRIED PORK WITH PEACHES

INGREDIENTS

Serves 4

400g/14oz/2 cups long grain rice
1 litre/1¾ pints/4 cups chicken stock
4 lean pork chops or loin pieces, about
  200g/7oz each
30ml/2 tbsp vegetable oil
30ml/2 tbsp dark rum or sherry
1 small onion, chopped
3 large ripe peaches
15ml/1 tbsp green peppercorns
15ml/1 tbsp white wine vinegar
salt and black pepper
flat leaf parsley, to garnish

NUTRITION NOTES

Per portion:
Energy	679Kcals/2852kJ
Fat	16.09g
Saturated fat	3.98g
Cholesterol	89.7mg
Fibre	1.84g

1 Place the rice in a large saucepan and cover with 900ml/1½ pints/ 3¾ cups chicken stock. Stir, bring to a simmer and cook uncovered for about 15 minutes. Switch off the heat, cover, and leave for 5 minutes. Season the pork. Heat a large metal frying pan and moisten the pork with 15ml/1 tbsp of the oil. Cook for about 12 minutes, turning once.

2 Transfer the meat to a warm plate. Pour off the excess fat from the pan and return to the heat. Allow the sediment to sizzle and brown, add the rum or sherry and loosen the sediment with a flat wooden spoon. Pour the pan contents over the meat, cover and keep warm. Wipe the pan clean.

3 Heat the remaining vegetable oil in the pan and soften the onion over a gentle heat.

4 Cover the peaches with boiling water to loosen the skins, then peel, slice and discard the stones.

5 Add the peaches and peppercorns to the onion and cook for about 3–4 minutes, until they begin to soften.

6 Add the remaining chicken stock and simmer briefly. Return the pork and meat juices to the pan, sharpen with vinegar, and season to taste. Serve the pork and peaches with the rice and garnish with flat leaf parsley.

COOK'S TIP
Unripe peaches are unsuitable. A can of sliced peaches may be used instead.

TURKISH LAMB AND APRICOT STEW

The chick-peas and almonds give a delightful crunchiness to this wholesome stew.

INGREDIENTS

Serves 4

1 large aubergine, cubed
30ml/2 tbsp sunflower oil
1 onion, chopped
1 garlic clove, crushed
5ml/1 tsp ground cinnamon
3 whole cloves
450g/1 lb boned leg of lean lamb, cubed
400g/14oz can chopped tomatoes
115g/4oz/²⁄₃ cup ready-to-eat dried apricots
115g/4oz/²⁄₃ cup canned chick-peas, drained
5ml/1 tsp clear honey
salt and black pepper
chopped fresh parsley, and 30ml/2 tbsp chopped almonds, fried in a little oil, to garnish
couscous, to serve

1 Place the aubergine in a colander, sprinkle with salt and leave for 30 minutes. Heat the oil in a flame-proof casserole, add the onion and garlic and fry for about 5 minutes.

2 Stir in the ground cinnamon and cloves and fry for about 1 minute. Add the lamb and cook for a further 5–6 minutes, stirring occasionally until well browned.

3 Rinse, drain and pat dry the aubergine, add to the pan and cook for about 3 minutes, stirring well. Add the tomatoes, 300ml/½ pint/1¼ cups water, the apricots and seasoning. Bring to the boil, then cover the pan and simmer gently for about 45 minutes.

4 Stir in the chick-peas and honey, and cook for a further 15–20 minutes, or until the lamb is tender. Serve the stew accompanied by couscous mixed with a little chopped parsley and garnished with the almonds.

NUTRITION NOTES

Per portion:

Energy	360 kcals/1512 kJ
Fat	17.05 g
Saturated fat	5.46g
Cholesterol	88.87mg
Fibre	6.16g

VARIATION
Grains are very healthy and full of proteins and vitamins. Chick-peas are no exception. This recipe could be adapted by substituting split-peas or lentils for chick-peas.

POULTRY AND GAME

Poultry and game are obvious choices for a low fat diet, as they are mostly very low in fat, and much of the fat they do contain is low in saturates. Chicken, always a favourite choice for family meals, is endlessly versatile and economical, and is well suited to low fat cooking methods. Turkey, also low fat, is now available in so many different cuts that it's almost interchangeable with chicken, and turkey mince can take the place of beef in healthy, savoury bakes and pasta dishes. For a change, introduce game into family meals, as it is particularly low in saturated fat and just as simple to cook as chicken. Even high fat poultry such as duck can be cooked in new ways to reduce fat – and add to the flavour.

JAMBALAYA

The perfect way to use up left-over cold meat – Jambalaya is a fast, easy-to-make fortifying meal for a hungry family.

INGREDIENTS

Serves 4

45ml/3 tbsp vegetable oil
1 onion, chopped
1 celery stick, chopped
½ red pepper, chopped
400g/14oz/2 cups long grain rice
1 litre/1¼ pints/4 cups chicken stock
15ml/1 tbsp tomato purée
3–4 shakes of Tabasco sauce
225g/8oz cold roast chicken without skin and bone or lean pork, thickly sliced
115g/4oz cooked sausage, such as Chorizo or Kabanos, sliced
75g/3oz/¾ cup frozen peas

1 Heat the oil in a heavy saucepan and add the onion, celery and pepper. Cook over a gentle heat until soft.

2 Add the rice, chicken stock, tomato purée and Tabasco sauce. Simmer uncovered for about 10 minutes.

VARIATION
Fish and shellfish are also good in a Jambalaya.

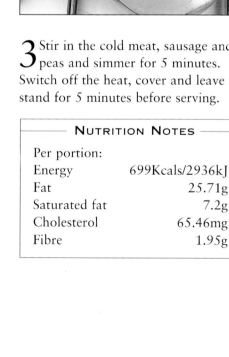

3 Stir in the cold meat, sausage and peas and simmer for 5 minutes. Switch off the heat, cover and leave to stand for 5 minutes before serving.

NUTRITION NOTES

Per portion:

Energy	699Kcals/2936kJ
Fat	25.71g
Saturated fat	7.2g
Cholesterol	65.46mg
Fibre	1.95g

GRILLED CHICKEN WITH HOT SALSA

This dish originates from
Mexico. Its hot and delicious
fruity flavours form the essence
of Tex-Mex cooking.

INGREDIENTS

Serves 4

*4 chicken breasts without skin and
  bone, about 175g/6oz each*
pinch of celery salt and cayenne pepper
30ml/2 tbsp vegetable oil
fresh coriander, to garnish
corn chips, to serve

For the salsa
275g/10oz watermelon
175g/6oz canteloupe melon
1 small red onion
1–2 green chillies
30ml/2 tbsp lime juice
60ml/4 tbsp chopped fresh coriander
pinch of salt

NUTRITION NOTES

Per portion:	
Energy	263Kcals/1106kJ
Fat	10.72g
Saturated fat	2.82g
Cholesterol	64.5mg
Fibre	0.72g

1 Preheat a moderate grill. Slash the
chicken breasts deeply to speed up
the cooking time.

2 Season the chicken with celery salt
and cayenne, brush with oil and
grill for about 15 minutes.

3 For the salsa, remove the rind and
seeds from the melons. Finely dice
the flesh and put it into a bowl.

4 Finely chop the onion, split the
chillies (discarding the seeds which
contain most of the heat) and chop.
Mix with the melon.

5 Add the lime juice and chopped
coriander, and season with a pinch
of salt. Turn the salsa out into a small
mixing bowl.

6 Arrange the grilled chicken on a
plate and serve with the salsa and a
handful of corn chips. Garnish with
sprigs of coriander.

COOK'S TIP
To capture the spirit of Tex-Mex
food, cook the chicken over a barbecue and eat shaded from the hot
summer sun.

MOROCCAN SPICED ROAST POUSSIN

INGREDIENTS

Serves 4

75g/3oz/1 cup cooked long grain rice
1 small onion, chopped finely
finely grated rind and juice of 1 lemon
30ml/2 tbsp chopped mint
45ml/3 tbsp chopped dried apricots
30ml/2 tbsp natural yogurt
10ml/2 tsp ground turmeric
10ml/2 tsp ground cumin
2 x 450g/1lb poussin
salt and black pepper
lemon slices and mint sprigs, to garnish

1 Preheat the oven to 200°C/400°F/
Gas 6. Mix together the rice, onion,
lemon rind, mint and apricots. Stir in
half each of the lemon juice, yogurt,
turmeric, cumin, and salt and pepper.

2 Stuff the poussin with the rice mixture at the neck end only. Any spare
stuffing can be served separately. Place
the poussin on a rack in a roasting tin.

3 Mix together the remaining lemon
juice, yogurt, turmeric and cumin,
then brush this over the poussin. Cover
loosely with foil and cook in the oven
for 30 minutes.

4 Remove the foil and roast for a
further 15 minutes, or until golden
brown and the juices run clear, not
pink, when pierced.

5 Cut the poussin in half with a sharp
knife or poultry shears, and serve
with the reserved rice. Garnish with
lemon slices and fresh mint.

NUTRITION NOTES

Per portion:
Energy	219Kcals/919kJ
Fat	6.02g
Saturated fat	1.87g
Cholesterol	71.55mg
Fibre	1.12g

STICKY GINGER CHICKEN

INGREDIENTS

Serves 4

30ml/2 tbsp lemon juice
30ml/2 tbsp light muscovado sugar
5ml/1 tsp grated fresh ginger root
10ml/2 tsp soy sauce
8 chicken drumsticks, skinned
black pepper

NUTRITION NOTES

Per portion:
Energy	162Kcals/679kJ
Fat	5.58g
Saturated fat	1.84g
Cholesterol	73mg
Fibre	0.08g

1 Mix together the lemon juice, sugar,
ginger, soy sauce and pepper.

2 With a sharp knife, slash the
chicken drumsticks about three
times through the thickest part, then
toss the chicken in the glaze.

3 Cook the chicken on a hot grill or
barbecue, turning occasionally and
brushing with the glaze, until the
chicken is golden and the juices run
clear, not pink, when pierced. Serve on
a bed of lettuce, with crusty bread.

STIR-FRIED SWEET AND SOUR CHICKEN

INGREDIENTS

Serves 4

275g/10oz Chinese egg noodles
30ml/2 tbsp sunflower oil
3 spring onions, chopped
1 garlic clove, crushed
2.5cm/1 in piece fresh root ginger,
    peeled and grated
5ml/1 tsp hot paprika
5ml/1 tsp ground coriander
3 chicken breasts without skin and
    bone, sliced
115g/4oz/1 cup mange-touts, topped
    and tailed
115g/4oz/1¼ cups baby corn, halved
225g/8oz/2¾ cups beansprouts
15ml/1 tbsp cornflour
45ml/3 tbsp soy sauce
45ml/3 tbsp lemon juice
15ml/1 tbsp sugar
45ml/3 tbsp chopped fresh coriander or
    spring onion, to garnish

1 Bring a large saucepan of salted water to the boil. Add the noodles and cook according to the manufacturer's instructions. Drain and cover.

2 Heat the oil. Add the spring onions and cook over a gentle heat. Mix in the next five ingredients, then stir-fry for about 3–4 minutes.

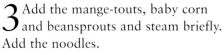

3 Add the mange-touts, baby corn and beansprouts and steam briefly. Add the noodles.

4 Combine the cornflour, soy sauce, lemon juice and sugar in a small bowl. Add to the wok and simmer briefly to thicken. Serve garnished with freshly chopped coriander or spring onion tops.

NUTRITION NOTES

Per portion:

Energy	528Kcals/2218kJ
Fat	15.44g
Saturated fat	2.32g
Cholesterol	48.38mg
Fibre	2.01g

COOK'S TIP

Large wok lids are cumbersome and can be difficult to store in a small kitchen. Consider placing a circle of greaseproof paper against the food surface to keep cooking juices in.

Be very careful when stir-frying dishes. Timing is very important and overcooking will ruin the flavour. When correctly done the food should be crispy. The high heat used in stir-frying will bring out the natural juices of the vegetables especially if they are fresh.

CHICKEN IN A CASHEW NUT SAUCE

This dish has a deliciously thick and nutty sauce.

INGREDIENTS

Serves 4

2 onions
30ml/2 tbsp tomato purée
50g/2oz/⅓ cup cashew nuts
7.5ml/1½ tsp garam masala
1 garlic clove, crushed
5ml/1 tsp chilli powder
15ml/1 tbsp lemon juice
1.5ml/¼ tsp turmeric
5ml/1 tsp salt
15ml/1 tbsp low fat natural yogurt
30ml/2 tbsp corn oil
15ml/1 tbsp chopped fresh coriander
15ml/1 tbsp sultanas
450g/1 lb chicken without skin and
    bone, cubed
175g/6oz/2½ cups button mushrooms
300ml/½ pint/1¼ cups water
sprig of coriander, to garnish

NUTRITION NOTES

Per portion:
Energy	280Kcals/1176kJ
Fat	14.64g
Saturated fat	2.87g
Cholesterol	64.84mg

1 Cut the onions into quarters and place in a food processor or blender and process for about 1 minute.

2 Add the tomato purée, cashew nuts, garam masala, garlic, chilli powder, lemon juice, turmeric, salt and yogurt to the processed onions.

3 Process all the ingredients in the food processor for a further 1–1½ minutes.

4 In a saucepan, heat the oil, lower the heat to medium and pour in the spice mixture from the food processor.

5 Fry the mixture for about 2 minutes, lowering the heat if necessary.

6 Add the fresh coriander, sultanas and chicken, and continue to stir-fry for a further 1 minute.

7 Add the mushrooms, pour in the water and bring to a simmer. Cover the pan and cook over a low heat for about 10 minutes. Check that the chicken is thoroughly cooked and the sauce is thick. Cook longer if necessary. Serve the chicken garnished with a sprig of coriander.

CHILLI CHICKEN COUSCOUS

Couscous is a very easy alternative to rice and makes a good base for all kinds of ingredients.

INGREDIENTS

Serves 4

225g/8oz/2 cups couscous
1 litre/1¼ pint/4 cups boiling water
5ml/1 tsp olive oil
400g/14oz chicken without skin and
    bone, diced
1 yellow pepper, seeded and sliced
2 large courgettes, sliced thickly
1 small green chilli, thinly sliced, or
    5ml/1 tsp chilli sauce
1 large tomato, diced
425g/15oz can chick-peas, drained
salt and black pepper
coriander or parsley sprigs to garnish

1 Place couscous in a large bowl and pour over boiling water. Cover and leave to stand for 30 minutes.

2 Heat the oil in a large, non-stick pan and stir fry the chicken quickly to seal, then reduce the heat.

3 Stir in the pepper, courgettes and chilli or sauce and cook for 10 minutes, until the vegetables are softened.

4 Stir in the tomato and chick-peas, then add the couscous. Adjust the seasoning and stir over a moderate heat until hot. Serve garnished with sprigs of fresh coriander or parsley.

NUTRITION NOTES

Per portion:

Energy	363Kcals/1525kJ
Fat	8.09g
Saturated fat	1.68g
Cholesterol	57mg
Fibre	4.38g

TURKEY BEAN BAKE

INGREDIENTS

Serves 4

1 medium aubergine, thinly sliced
15ml/1 tbsp olive oil, for brushing
450g/1 lb turkey breast, diced
1 medium onion, chopped
400g/14oz can chopped tomatoes
425g/15oz can red kidney beans,
    drained
15ml/1 tbsp paprika
15ml/1 tbsp fresh chopped thyme, or
    5ml/1 tsp dried
5ml/1 tsp chilli sauce
350g/12oz/1½ cups Greek-style yogurt
2.5ml/½ tsp grated nutmeg
salt and black pepper

1 Preheat the oven to 190°C/375°F/ Gas 5. Arrange the aubergine in a colander and sprinkle with salt.

2 Leave the aubergine for 30 minutes, then rinse and pat dry. Brush a non-stick pan with oil and fry the aubergine in batches, turning once, until golden.

3 Remove aubergine, add the turkey and onion to the pan, then cook until lightly browned. Stir in the tomatoes, beans, paprika, thyme, chilli sauce, and salt and pepper. In a separate bowl, mix together the yogurt and grated nutmeg.

4 Layer the meat and aubergine in an ovenproof dish, finishing with aubergine. Spread over the yogurt and bake for 50–60 minutes, until golden.

NUTRITION NOTES

Per portion:

Energy	370Kcals/1555kJ
Fat	13.72g
Saturated fat	5.81g
Cholesterol	66.5mg
Fibre	7.38g

SPICY MASALA CHICKEN

These chicken pieces are grilled and have a sweet-and-sour taste. They can be served cold with a salad and rice, or hot with mashed potatoes.

INGREDIENTS

Serves 6

12 chicken thighs without skin
90ml/6 tbsp lemon juice
5ml/1 tsp grated fresh root ginger
1 garlic clove, crushed
5ml/1 tsp crushed dried red chillies
5ml/1 tsp salt
5ml/1 tsp soft brown sugar
30ml/2 tbsp clear honey
30ml/2 tbsp chopped fresh coriander
1 green chilli, finely chopped
30ml/2 tbsp sunflower oil
sliced chilli, to garnish

1 Prick the chicken thighs with a fork, rinse, pat dry and set aside in a large bowl.

2 In a large mixing bowl, mix together the lemon juice, ginger, garlic, crushed dried red chillies, salt, sugar and honey.

3 Transfer the chicken thighs to the spice mixture and coat well. Set aside for about 45 minutes.

4 Preheat the grill to medium. Add the fresh coriander and chopped green chilli to the chicken thighs and place them on a flameproof dish.

5 Pour any remaining marinade over the chicken and baste with the oil, using a pastry brush.

6 Grill the chicken thighs under the preheated grill for about 15–20 minutes, turning and basting occasionally, until cooked through and browned.

7 Transfer to a serving dish and garnish with the sliced chilli.

NUTRITION NOTES	
Per portion:	
Energy	189Kcals/795kJ
Fat	9.2g
Saturated fat	2.31g
Cholesterol	73mg

TANDOORI CHICKEN

This popular Indian chicken dish is traditionally cooked in a clay oven called a tandoor. Although the authentic tandoori flavour is very difficult to achieve in conventional ovens, this version still makes a very tasty dish.

INGREDIENTS

Serves 4

4 chicken quarters without skin
175ml/6fl oz/¾ cup low fat natural yogurt
5ml/1 tsp garam masala
5ml/1 tsp grated fresh root ginger
1 garlic clove, crushed
7.5ml/1½ tsp chilli powder
1.5ml/¼ tsp turmeric
5ml/1 tsp ground coriander
15ml/1 tbsp lemon juice
5ml/1 tsp salt
a few drops of red food colouring
30ml/2 tbsp corn oil

For the garnish
mixed salad leaves
lime slices
chillies
tomato quarters

1 Rinse and pat dry the chicken quarters. Make two slits into the flesh of each piece, place in a dish and set aside.

2 Mix together the yogurt, garam masala, ginger, garlic, chilli powder, turmeric, ground coriander, lemon juice, salt, red colouring and oil, and beat so that all the ingredients are mixed together well.

3 Cover the chicken quarters with the spice mixture and leave to marinate for about 3 hours.

4 Preheat the oven to 240°C/475°F/Gas 9. Transfer the chicken pieces to an ovenproof dish.

5 Bake in the preheated oven for about 20–25 minutes or until the chicken is cooked right through and browned on top.

6 Remove from the oven, transfer on to a serving dish, and garnish with the salad leaves, lime and tomato.

NUTRITION NOTES

Per portion:

Energy	242Kcals/1018kJ
Fat	10.64g
Saturated fat	2.74g
Cholesterol	81.9mg

TURKEY PASTITSIO

A traditional Greek pastitsio is a rich, high fat dish made with beef mince, but this lighter version is just as tasty.

INGREDIENTS

Serves 4–6

450g/1 lb lean minced turkey
1 large onion, finely chopped
60ml/4 tbsp tomato purée
250ml/8 fl oz/1 cup red wine or stock
5ml/1 tsp ground cinnamon
300g/11oz/2½ cups macaroni
300ml/½ pint/1¼ cups skimmed milk
25g/1oz/2 tbsp sunflower margarine
25g/1oz/3 tbsp plain flour
5ml/1 tsp grated nutmeg
2 tomatoes, sliced
60ml/4 tbsp wholemeal breadcrumbs
salt and black pepper
green salad, to serve

1 Preheat the oven to 220°C/425°F/ Gas 7. Fry the turkey and onion in a non-stick pan without fat, stirring until lightly browned.

2 Stir in the tomato purée, red wine or stock and cinnamon. Season, then cover and simmer for 5 minutes.

3 Cook the macaroni in boiling, salted water until just tender, then drain. Layer with the meat mixture in a wide ovenproof dish.

4 Place the milk, margarine and flour in a saucepan and whisk over a moderate heat until thickened and smooth. Add the nutmeg, and salt and pepper to taste.

5 Pour the sauce evenly over the pasta and meat. Arrange the tomato slices on top and sprinkle lines of breadcrumbs over the surface.

6 Bake for 30–35 minutes, or until golden brown and bubbling. Serve hot with a green salad.

NUTRITION NOTES

Per portion:

Energy	566Kcals/2382kJ
Fat	8.97g
Saturated fat	1.76g
Cholesterol	57.06mg
Fibre	4.86g

TUSCAN CHICKEN

This simple peasant casserole has all the flavours of traditional Tuscan ingredients. The wine can be replaced by chicken stock.

INGREDIENTS

Serves 4
8 chicken thighs, skinned
5ml/1 tsp olive oil
1 medium onion, sliced thinly
2 red peppers, seeded and sliced
1 garlic clove, crushed
300ml/ ½ pint/1¼ cups passata
150ml/¼ pint/⅔ cup dry white wine
large sprig fresh oregano, or 5ml/1 tsp
  dried oregano
400g/14oz can cannelini beans, drained
45ml/3 tbsp fresh breadcrumbs
salt and black pepper

1 Fry the chicken in the oil in a non-stick or heavy pan until golden brown. Remove and keep hot. Add the onion and peppers to the pan and gently sauté until softened, but not brown. Stir in the garlic.

2 Add the chicken, passata, wine and oregano. Season well, bring to the boil then cover the pan tightly.

3 Lower the heat and simmer gently, stirring occasionally for 30–35 minutes or until the chicken is tender and the juices run clear, not pink, when pierced with the point of a knife.

4 Stir in the cannelini beans and simmer for a further 5 minutes until heated through. Sprinkle with the breadcrumbs and cook under a hot grill until golden brown.

NUTRITION NOTES

Per portion:

Energy	248Kcals/1045kJ
Fat	7.53g
Saturated fat	2.06g
Cholesterol	73mg
Fibre	4.03g

MANDARIN SESAME DUCK

Duck is a high fat meat but it is possible to get rid of a good proportion of the fat cooked in this way. (If you remove the skin completely, the meat can be dry.) For a special occasion, duck breasts are a good choice, but they are more expensive.

INGREDIENTS

Serves 4

4 duck leg or boneless breast portions
30ml/2 tbsp light soy sauce
45ml/3 tbsp clear honey
15ml/1 tbsp sesame seeds
4 mandarin oranges
5ml/1 tsp cornflour
salt and black pepper

1 Preheat the oven to 180°C/350°F/ Gas 4. Prick the duck skin all over. Slash the breast skin diagonally at intervals with a sharp knife.

2 Place the duck on a rack in a roasting tin and roast for 1 hour. Mix 15ml/1 tbsp soy sauce with 30ml/2 tbsp honey and brush over the duck. Sprinkle with sesame seeds. Roast for 15–20 minutes, until golden brown.

3 Meanwhile, grate the rind from one mandarin and squeeze the juice from two. Mix in the cornflour, then stir in the remaining soy sauce and honey. Heat, stirring, until thickened and clear. Season. Peel and slice the remaining mandarins. Serve the duck, with the mandarin slices and the sauce.

NUTRITION NOTES

Per portion:

Energy	624Kcals/2621kJ
Fat	48.63g
Saturated fat	12.99g
Cholesterol	256mg
Fibre	0.95g

MINTY YOGURT CHICKEN

INGREDIENTS

Serves 4

8 chicken thigh portions, skinned
15ml/1 tbsp clear honey
30ml/2 tbsp lime or lemon juice
30ml/2 tbsp natural yogurt
60ml/4 tbsp chopped fresh mint
salt and black pepper

1 Slash the chicken flesh at intervals with a sharp knife. Place in a bowl.

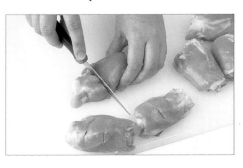

2 Mix the lime or honey, lemon juice, yogurt, seasoning and half the mint.

3 Spoon the marinade over the chicken and leave to marinate for 30 minutes. Line the grill pan with foil and cook the chicken under a moderately hot grill until thoroughly cooked and golden brown, turning the chicken occasionally during cooking.

4 Sprinkle with remaining mint, serve with potatoes and tomato salad.

NUTRITION NOTES

Per portion:

Energy	171Kcals/719kJ
Fat	6.74g
Saturated fat	2.23g
Cholesterol	97.90mg
Fibre	0.01g

TURKEY SPIRALS

These little spirals may look difficult, but they're very simple to make, and a very good way to pep up plain turkey.

INGREDIENTS

Serves 4

4 thinly sliced turkey breast steaks,
  about 90g/3½oz each
20ml/4 tsp tomato purée
15g/½oz/½ cup large basil leaves
1 garlic clove, crushed
15ml/1 tbsp skimmed milk
30ml/2 tbsp wholemeal flour
salt and black pepper
passata or fresh tomato sauce and
  pasta with fresh basil, to serve

1 Place the turkey steaks on a board. If too thick, flatten them slightly by beating with a rolling pin.

2 Spread each turkey breast steak with tomato purée, then top with a few leaves of basil, a little crushed garlic, and salt and pepper.

3 Roll up firmly around the filling and secure with a cocktail stick. Brush with milk and sprinkle with flour to coat lightly.

4 Place the spirals on a foil-lined grill-pan. Cook under a medium-hot grill for 15–20 minutes, turning them occasionally, until thoroughly cooked. Serve hot, sliced with a spoonful or two of passata or fresh tomato sauce and pasta, sprinkled with fresh basil.

> COOK'S TIP
> When flattening the turkey steaks with a rolling pin, place them between two sheets of cling film.

NUTRITION NOTES

Per portion:

Energy	123Kcals/518kJ
Fat	1.21g
Saturated fat	0.36g
Cholesterol	44.17mg
Fibre	0.87g

CARIBBEAN CHICKEN KEBABS

These kebabs have a rich, sunshine Caribbean flavour and the marinade keeps them moist without the need for oil. Serve with a colourful salad and rice.

INGREDIENTS

Serves 4
500g/1¼ lb boneless chicken breasts, skinned
finely grated rind of 1 lime
30ml/2 tbsp lime juice
15ml/1 tbsp rum or sherry
15ml/1 tbsp light muscovado sugar
5ml/1 tsp ground cinnamon
2 mangoes, peeled and cubed
rice and salad, to serve

1 Cut the chicken into bite-sized chunks and place in a bowl with the lime rind and juice, rum, sugar and cinnamon. Toss well, cover and leave to stand for 1 hour.

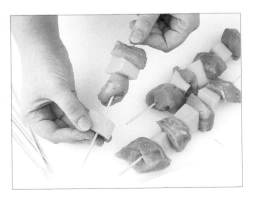

2 Save the juices and thread the chicken on to four wooden skewers, alternating with the mango cubes.

3 Cook the skewers under a hot grill or barbecue for 8–10 minutes, turning occasionally and basting with the juices, until the chicken is tender and golden brown. Serve at once with rice and salad.

COOK'S TIP
The rum or sherry adds a lovely rich flavour, but it is optional so can be omitted if you prefer to make the dish more economical.

NUTRITION NOTES

Per portion:

Energy	218Kcals/918kJ
Fat	4.17g
Saturated fat	1.33g
Cholesterol	53.75mg
Fibre	2.26g

OAT-CRUSTED CHICKEN WITH SAGE

Oats make a good coating for savoury foods, and offer a good way to add extra fibre.

INGREDIENTS

Serves 4

45ml/3 tbsp skimmed milk
10ml/2 tsp English mustard
40g/1½ oz/½ cup rolled oats
45ml/3 tbsp chopped sage leaves
8 chicken thighs or drumsticks, skinned
115g/4oz/½ cup low fat fromage frais
5ml/1 tsp wholegrain mustard
salt and black pepper
fresh sage leaves, to garnish

1 Preheat the oven to 200°C/400°F/ Gas 6. Mix together the milk and English mustard.

2 Mix the oats with 30ml/2 tbsp of the sage and the seasoning on a plate. Brush the chicken with the milk and press into the oats to coat evenly.

3 Place the chicken on a baking sheet and bake for about 40 minutes, or until the juices run clear, not pink, when pierced through the thickest part.

4 Meanwhile, mix together the low fat fromage frais, mustard, remaining sage and seasoning, then serve with the chicken. Garnish the chicken with fresh sage and serve hot or cold.

COOK'S TIP
If fresh sage is not available, choose another fresh herb such as thyme or parsley, instead of using a dried alternative.

NUTRITION NOTES

Per portion:

Energy	214Kcals/898kJ
Fat	6.57g
Saturated fat	1.81g
Cholesterol	64.64mg
Fibre	0.74g

CHICKEN IN CREAMY ORANGE SAUCE

This sauce is deceptively creamy
– in fact it is made with low fat
fromage frais, which is virtually
fat-free. The brandy adds a
richer flavour, but is optional –
omit it if you prefer and use
orange juice alone.

INGREDIENTS

Serves 4
8 chicken thighs or drumsticks, skinned
45ml/3 tbsp brandy
300ml/½ pint/1¼ cups orange juice
3 spring onions, chopped
10ml/2 tsp cornflour
90ml/6 tbsp low fat fromage frais
salt and black pepper

1 Fry the chicken pieces without fat in
a non-stick or heavy pan, turning
until evenly browned.

2 Stir in the brandy, orange juice and
spring onions. Bring to the boil,
then cover and simmer for 15 minutes,
or until the chicken is tender and the
juices run clear, not pink, when pierced.

3 Blend the cornflour with a little
water then mix into the fromage
frais. Stir this into the sauce and stir
over a moderate heat until boiling.

4 Adjust the seasoning and serve with
boiled rice or pasta and green salad.

COOK'S TIP
Cornflour stabilises the fromage
frais and helps prevent it curdling.

NUTRITION NOTES

Per portion:
Energy	227Kcals/951kJ
Fat	6.77g
Saturated fat	2.23g
Cholesterol	87.83mg
Fibre	0.17g

AUTUMN PHEASANT

Pheasant is worth buying as it is low in fat, full of flavour and never dry when cooked like this.

INGREDIENTS

Serves 4

1 oven-ready pheasant
2 small onions, quartered
3 celery sticks, thickly sliced
2 red eating apples, thickly sliced
120ml / 4 fl oz / ½ cup stock
15ml / 1 tbsp clear honey
30ml / 2 tbsp Worcestershire sauce
grated nutmeg
30ml / 2 tbsp toasted hazelnuts
salt and black pepper

1 Preheat the oven to 180°C/350°F/ Gas 4. Fry the pheasant without fat in a non-stick pan, turning occasionally until golden. Remove and keep hot.

2 Fry the onions and celery in the pan to brown lightly. Spoon into a casserole and place the pheasant on top. Tuck the apple slices around it.

3 Spoon over the stock, honey and Worcestershire sauce. Sprinkle with nutmeg, salt and pepper, cover and bake for 1¼ –1½ hours or until tender. Sprinkle with nuts and serve hot.

NUTRITION NOTES

Per portion:

Energy	387Kcals/1624kJ
Fat	16.97g
Saturated fat	4.28g
Cholesterol	126mg
Fibre	2.72g

CIDER BAKED RABBIT

Rabbit is a low fat meat and an economical choice for family meals. Chicken joints may be used as an alternative.

INGREDIENTS

Serves 4

450g / 1 lb rabbit joints
15ml / 1 tbsp plain flour
5ml / 1 tsp dry mustard powder
3 medium leeks, thickly sliced
250ml / 8 fl oz / 1 cup dry cider
2 sprigs rosemary
salt and black pepper
fresh rosemary, to garnish

1 Preheat the oven to 180°C/350°F/ Gas 4. Place the rabbit joints in a bowl and sprinkle over the flour and mustard powder. Toss to coat evenly.

2 Arrange the rabbit in one layer in a wide casserole. Blanch the leeks in boiling water, then drain and add to the casserole.

3 Add the cider, rosemary and season- ing, cover, then bake for 1–1¼ hours, or until the rabbit is tender. Garnish with fresh rosemary and serve with jacket potatoes and vegetables.

NUTRITION NOTES

Per portion:

Energy	162Kcals/681kJ
Fat	4.22g
Saturated fat	1.39g
Cholesterol	62.13mg
Fibre	1.27g

CHINESE-STYLE CHICKEN SALAD

INGREDIENTS

Serves 4

4 boneless chicken breasts, about
175g/6oz each
60ml/4 tbsp dark soy sauce
pinch of Chinese five-spice powder
a good squeeze of lemon juice
½ cucumber, peeled and cut into
matchsticks
5ml/1 tsp salt
45ml/3 tbsp sunflower oil
30ml/2 tbsp sesame oil
15ml/1 tbsp sesame seeds
30ml/2 tbsp dry sherry
2 carrots, cut into matchsticks
8 spring onions, shredded
75g/3oz/1 cup beansprouts

For the sauce

60ml/4 tbsp crunchy peanut butter
10ml/2 tsp lemon juice
10ml/2 tsp sesame oil
1.5ml/¼ tsp hot chilli powder
1 spring onion, finely chopped

1 Place the chicken portions in a large saucepan and just cover with water. Add 15ml/1 tbsp of the soy sauce, the Chinese five-spice powder and lemon juice, cover and bring to the boil, then simmer for about 20 minutes.

2 Meanwhile, place the cucumber matchsticks in a colander, sprinkle with the salt and cover with a plate with a weight on top. Leave to drain for about 30 minutes – set the colander in a bowl or on a deep plate to catch any drips that may fall.

3 Lift out the poached chicken with a slotted spoon and leave until cool enough to handle. Remove and discard the skins and bash the chicken lightly with a rolling pin to loosen the fibres. Slice into thin strips and reserve.

4 Heat the oils in a large frying pan or wok. Add the sesame seeds, fry for 30 seconds and then stir in the remaining 45ml/3 tbsp soy sauce and the sherry. Add the carrots and stir-fry for about 2–3 minutes, until just tender. Remove the wok or pan from the heat and reserve until required.

5 Rinse the cucumber well, pat dry with kitchen paper and place in a bowl. Add the spring onions, beansprouts, cooked carrots, pan juices and shredded chicken, and mix together. Transfer to a shallow dish. Cover and chill for about 1 hour, turning the mixture in the juices once or twice.

6 For the sauce, cream the peanut butter with the lemon juice, sesame oil and chilli powder, adding a little hot water to form a paste, then stir in the spring onion. Arrange the chicken mixture on a serving dish and serve with the peanut sauce.

NUTRITION NOTES	
Per portion:	
Energy	534Kcals/2241kJ
Fat	36.86g
Saturated fat	4.96g
Cholesterol	68.8mg
Fibre	2.91g

CHICKEN BIRYANI

INGREDIENTS

Serves 4

275g/10oz/1½ cups basmati rice, rinsed
2.5ml/½ tsp salt
5 whole cardamom pods
2–3 whole cloves
1 cinnamon stick
45ml/3 tbsp sunflower oil
3 onions, sliced
675g/1½ lb chicken breasts without
   skin and bone, cubed
1.5ml/¼ tsp ground cloves
5 cardamom pods, seeds removed and
   ground
1.5ml/¼ tsp hot chilli powder
5ml/1 tsp ground cumin
5ml/1 tsp ground coriander
2.5ml/½ tsp ground black pepper
3 garlic cloves, finely chopped
5ml/1 tsp finely chopped fresh root
   ginger
juice of 1 lemon
4 tomatoes, sliced
30ml/2 tbsp chopped fresh coriander
150ml/¼ pint/⅔ cup low fat natural
   yogurt
2.5ml/½ tsp saffron strands soaked in
   10ml/2 tsp hot skimmed milk
low fat natural yogurt, 45ml/3 tbsp
   toasted flaked almonds and fresh
   coriander leaves, to garnish

3 Transfer the chicken mixture to an ovenproof casserole and lay the tomatoes on top. Sprinkle over the fresh coriander, spoon over the yogurt, and top with the drained rice.

2 Heat the oil in a frying pan and fry the onions for about 8 minutes, until browned. Add the chicken followed by all the ground spices, the garlic, ginger and lemon juice. Stir-fry for a further 5 minutes.

NUTRITION NOTES	
Per portion:	
Energy	650Kcals/2730kJ
Fat	21.43g
Saturated fat	3.62g
Cholesterol	74.11mg
Fibre	2.95g

4 Drizzle the saffron strands and skimmed milk over the rice and pour over 150ml/¼ pint/⅔ cup of water.

1 Preheat the oven to 190°C/375°F/ Gas 5. Bring a saucepan of water to the boil and add the rice, salt, cardamom pods, cloves and cinnamon stick. Boil for about 2 minutes and then drain, leaving the whole spices in the rice.

5 Cover with a tight-fitting lid and bake in the oven for about 1 hour. Transfer to a warmed serving platter and remove the whole spices from the rice. Garnish with low fat natural yogurt, toasted almonds and fresh coriander leaves.

STIR-FRIED TURKEY WITH MANGE-TOUTS

A quick and easy dish served with saffron rice.

INGREDIENTS

Serves 4
30ml/2 tbsp sesame oil
90ml/6 tbsp lemon juice
1 garlic clove, crushed
1cm/½ in piece fresh root ginger, grated
5ml/1 tsp clear honey
450g/1 lb lean turkey fillets, cut into
    strips
115g/4oz/1 cup mange-touts, trimmed
30ml/2 tbsp groundnut oil
50g/2oz/⅓ cup cashew nuts
6 spring onions, cut into strips
225g/8oz can water chestnuts, drained
    and thinly sliced
pinch of salt
saffron rice, to serve

1 Mix together the sesame oil, lemon juice, garlic, ginger and honey in a shallow non-metallic dish. Add the turkey and mix well. Cover and leave to marinate for about 3–4 hours.

2 Blanch the mange-touts in boiling salted water for 1 minute. Drain and refresh under cold running water.

3 Drain the marinade from the turkey strips and reserve the marinade. Heat the groundnut oil in a wok or large frying pan, add the cashew nuts, and stir-fry for about 1–2 minutes.

NUTRITION NOTES	
Per portion:	
Energy	311Kcals/1307kJ
Fat	18.51g
Saturated fat	2.9g
Cholesterol	55.12mg

4 Remove the cashew nuts from the wok or frying pan using a slotted spoon and set aside.

5 Add the turkey and stir-fry for about 3–4 minutes, until golden brown. Add the mange-touts, spring onions and water chestnuts with the reserved marinade. Cook until the turkey is tender and the sauce is bubbling and hot. Add salt to taste. Stir in the cashew nuts and serve at once with saffron rice.

HOT CHICKEN CURRY

This curry has a flavourful thick sauce, and includes red and green peppers for extra colour. Serve with wholemeal chapatis or plain boiled rice.

INGREDIENTS

Serves 4

30ml/2 tbsp corn oil
1.5ml/¼ tsp fenugreek seeds
1.5ml/¼ tsp onion seeds
2 onions, chopped
1 garlic clove, crushed
2.5ml/½ tsp grated fresh root ginger
5ml/1 tsp ground coriander
5ml/1 tsp chilli powder
5ml/1 tsp salt
400g/14oz can tomatoes
30ml/2 tbsp lemon juice
350g/12oz chicken without skin and
    bone, cubed
30ml/2 tbsp chopped fresh coriander
3 green chillies, chopped
½ red pepper, cut into chunks
½ green pepper, cut into chunks
fresh coriander leaves, to garnish

1 Heat the oil in a medium saucepan, and fry the fenugreek and onion seeds until they turn a shade darker. Add the onions, garlic and ginger and fry for about 5 minutes until the onions are golden. Lower the heat to very low.

COOK'S TIP
For a milder version of this delicious curry, simply omit some or all of the fresh green chillies.

2 Meanwhile, in a separate bowl, mix together the ground coriander, chilli powder, salt, tomatoes and lemon juice.

3 Pour this mixture into the pan and turn up the heat to medium. Stir-fry for about 3 minutes.

NUTRITION NOTES

Per portion:

Energy	205Kcals/861kJ
Fat	9.83g
Saturated fat	2.03g
Cholesterol	48.45mg

4 Add the chicken and stir-fry for about 5–7 minutes. Take care not to overcook the chicken.

5 Add the fresh coriander, green chillies and the pepper chunks. Lower the heat, cover, and simmer for about 10 minutes until cooked. Serve hot, garnished with fresh coriander leaves.

FISH AND SEAFOOD

Fish is ideally designed for healthy, quick family meals. Most types of fish are very low in fat and high in protein, and even oily fish is high in essential fatty acids. Unlike meat, fish never needs long, slow cooking to tenderise it, so dinner can be on the table in less than half an hour! Tempt any reluctant fish eaters with wonderful exotic flavours – a spicy Moroccan Tagine perhaps, or a hearty Cod Creole to pep up the taste buds. Fussy young fish-eaters are sure to clear their plate of Hoki Balls in Tomato Sauce or Tuna and Corn Fish Cakes, or will even try mackerel if it is presented without risk of bones, on fun-to-eat kebabs.

PRAWNS WITH VEGETABLES

This is a light and nutritious dish. It is excellent served either on a bed of lettuce leaves, with plain boiled rice or wholemeal chapatis for a healthy meal.

INGREDIENTS

Serves 4

30ml/2 tbsp chopped fresh coriander
5ml/1 tsp salt
2 green chillies, seeded if required
45ml/3 tbsp lemon juice
30ml/2 tbsp vegetable oil
20 cooked king prawns, peeled
1 courgette, thickly sliced
1 onion, cut into 8 chunks
8 cherry tomatoes
8 baby corn
mixed salad leaves, to serve

NUTRITION NOTES

Per portion:

Energy	109Kcals/458kJ
Fat	6.47g
Saturated fat	0.85g
Cholesterol	29.16mg

1 Place the chopped coriander, salt, green chillies, lemon juice and oil in a food processor or blender and process for a few seconds.

2 Remove the paste from the processor and transfer to a mixing bowl.

3 Add the peeled prawns to the paste and stir to make sure that all the prawns are well coated. Set aside to marinate for about 30 minutes.

4 Preheat the grill to very hot, then turn the heat down to medium.

5 Arrange the vegetables and prawns alternately on four skewers. When all the skewers are ready place them under the preheated grill for about 5–7 minutes until cooked and browned.

6 Serve immediately on a bed of mixed salad leaves.

COOK'S TIP
King prawns are a luxury, but worth choosing for a very special dinner party. For a more economical variation, substitute the king prawns with 450g/1 lb/2½ cups peeled prawns.

GRILLED FISH FILLETS

Fish can be grilled beautifully without sacrificing any flavour. This recipe uses a minimum amount of oil to baste the fish.

INGREDIENTS

Serves 4

4 flatfish fillets, such as plaice, sole or flounder, about 115g/4oz each
1 garlic clove, crushed
5ml/1 tsp garam masala
5ml/1 tsp chilli powder
1.5ml/¼ tsp turmeric
2.5ml/½ tsp salt
15ml/1 tbsp finely chopped fresh coriander
15ml/1 tbsp vegetable oil
30ml/2 tbsp lemon juice

1 Line a flameproof dish or grill tray with foil. Rinse and pat dry the fish fillets and put them on the foil-lined dish or tray.

2 In a small bowl, mix together the garlic, garam masala, chilli powder, turmeric, salt, fresh coriander, oil and lemon juice.

3 Using a pastry brush, baste the fish fillets evenly all over with the spice and lemon juice mixture.

COOK'S TIP
Although frozen fish can be used for this dish always try to buy fresh. It is more flavoursome.

4 Preheat the grill to very hot, then lower the heat to medium. Grill the fillets for about 10 minutes, turning as necessary and basting occasionally, until they are cooked right through.

5 Serve immediately with an attractive garnish. This could include grated carrot, tomato quarters and lime slices, if you wish.

NUTRITION NOTES

Per portion:

Energy	143Kcals/599kJ
Fat	5.63g
Saturated fat	0.84g
Cholesterol	47.25mg

CRUNCHY-TOPPED COD

Colourful and quick to cook, this is ideal for weekday meals.

INGREDIENTS

Serves 4
4 pieces cod fillet, about 115g/4oz
*   each, skinned*
2 medium tomatoes, sliced
50g/2oz/1 cup fresh wholemeal bread-
*   crumbs*
30ml/2 tbsp chopped fresh parsley
finely grated rind and juice of ½ lemon
5 ml/1 tsp sunflower oil
salt and ground black pepper

1 Preheat the oven to 200°C/400°F/
Gas 6. Arrange the cod fillets in a
wide, ovenproof dish.

2 Arrange the tomato slices on top.
Mix together the breadcrumbs,
fresh parsley, lemon rind and juice and
the oil with seasoning to taste.

3 Spoon the crumb mixture evenly
over the fish, then bake for 15–20
minutes. Serve hot.

NUTRITION NOTES

Per portion:
Energy	130Kcals/546kJ
Fat	2.06g
Saturated fat	0.32g
Cholesterol	52.9mg
Fibre	1.4g

SPECIAL FISH PIE

This fish pie is colourful, healthy
and best of all very easy to
make. For a more economical
version, omit the prawns and
replace with more fish fillet.

INGREDIENTS

Serves 4
350g/12oz haddock fillet, skinned
30ml/2 tbsp cornflour
115g/4oz cooked, peeled prawns
198g/7oz can sweetcorn, drained
75g/3oz frozen peas
150ml/¼ pint/⅔ cup skimmed milk
150g/5oz/⅔ cup low fat fromage frais
75g/3oz fresh wholemeal breadcrumbs
40g/1½oz/½ cup grated reduced fat
*   Cheddar cheese*
salt and black pepper

1 Preheat the oven to 190°C/375°F/
Gas 5. Cut the haddock into bite-
sized pieces and toss in cornflour to
coat evenly.

2 Place the fish, prawns, sweetcorn
and peas in an ovenproof dish. Beat
together the milk, fromage frais and
seasonings, then pour into the dish.

3 Mix together the breadcrumbs and
grated cheese then spoon evenly
over the top. Bake for 25–30 minutes,
or until golden brown. Serve hot with
fresh vegetables.

NUTRITION NOTES

Per portion:
Energy	290Kcals/1218kJ
Fat	4.87g
Saturated fat	2.1g
Cholesterol	63.91mg
Fibre	2.61g

Haddock and Broccoli Chowder

A warming main-meal soup for hearty appetites.

INGREDIENTS

Serves 4
4 spring onions, sliced
450g/1 lb new potatoes, diced
300ml/½ pint/1¼ cups fish stock or
    water
300ml/½ pint/1¼ cups skimmed milk
1 bay leaf
225g/8oz/2 cups broccoli florets, sliced
450g/1 lb smoked haddock fillets,
    skinned
198g/7oz can sweetcorn, drained
black pepper
chopped spring onions, to garnish

1 Place the spring onions and potatoes in a large saucepan and add the stock, milk and bay leaf. Bring the soup to the boil, then cover the pan and simmer for 10 minutes.

2 Add the broccoli to the pan. Cut the fish into bite-sized chunks and add to the pan with the sweetcorn.

3 Season the soup well with black pepper, then cover the pan and simmer for a further 5 minutes, or until the fish is cooked through. Remove the bay leaf and scatter over the spring onion. Serve hot, with crusty bread.

COOK'S TIP
When new potatoes are not available, old ones can be used, but choose a waxy variety which will not disintegrate.

NUTRITION NOTES

Per portion:
Energy	268Kcals/1124kJ
Fat	2.19g
Saturated fat	0.27g
Cholesterol	57.75mg
Fibre	3.36g

MOROCCAN FISH TAGINE

Tagine is actually the name of the large Moroccan cooking pot used for this type of cooking, but you can use an ordinary casserole intead.

INGREDIENTS

Serves 4

2 garlic cloves, crushed
30ml/2 tbsp ground cumin
30ml/2 tbsp paprika
1 small red chilli (optional)
30ml/2 tbsp tomato purée
60ml/4 tbsp lemon juice
4 cutlets of whiting or cod, about
*   175g/6oz each*
350g/12oz tomatoes, sliced
2 green peppers, seeded and
*   thinly sliced*
salt and black pepper
chopped fresh coriander, to garnish

1 Mix together the garlic, cumin, paprika, chilli, tomato purée and lemon juice. Spread this mixture over the fish, then cover and chill for about 30 minutes to let the flavour penetrate.

2 Preheat the oven to 200°C/400°F/ Gas 6. Arrange half of the tomatoes and peppers in a baking dish.

3 Cover with the fish, in one layer, then arrange the remaining tomatoes and pepper on top. Cover the baking dish with foil and bake for about 45 minutes, until the fish is tender. Sprinkle with chopped coriander or parsley to serve.

COOK'S TIP
If you are preparing this dish for a dinner party, it can be assembled completely and stored in the fridge, ready to bake when needed.

NUTRITION NOTES	
Per portion:	
Energy	203Kcals/855kJ
Fat	3.34g
Saturated fat	0.29g
Cholesterol	80.5mg
Fibre	2.48g

SEAFOOD PILAF

This all-in-one-pan main course is a satisfying meal for any day of the week. For a special meal, substitute dry white wine for the orange juice.

INGREDIENTS

Serves 4
10ml/2 tsp olive oil
250g/9oz/1¼ cups long grain rice
5ml/1 tsp ground turmeric
1 red pepper, seeded and diced
1 small onion, finely chopped
2 medium courgettes, sliced
150g/5oz/2 cups button mushrooms, halved
350ml/12 fl oz/1½ cups fish or chicken stock
150ml/¼ pint/⅔ cup orange juice
350g/12oz white fish fillets
12 fresh mussels in the shell (or cooked shelled mussels)
salt and ground black pepper
grated rind of 1 orange, to garnish

1 Heat the oil in a large, non-stick pan and fry the rice and turmeric over a low heat for about 1 minute.

2 Add the pepper, onion, courgettes, and mushrooms. Stir in the stock and orange juice. Bring to the boil.

3 Reduce the heat and add the fish. Cover and simmer gently for about 15 minutes, until the rice is tender and the liquid absorbed. Stir in the mussels and heat thoroughly. Adjust the seasoning, sprinkle with orange rind and serve hot.

NUTRITION NOTES

Per portion:
Energy	370Kcals/1555kJ
Fat	3.84g
Saturated fat	0.64g
Cholesterol	61.25mg
Fibre	2.08g

SALMON PASTA WITH PARSLEY SAUCE

INGREDIENTS

Serves 4
450g/1 lb salmon fillet, skinned
225g/8oz/3 cups pasta, such as penne or twists
175g/6oz cherry tomatoes, halved
150ml/¼ pint/⅔ cup low fat crème fraîche
45ml/3 tbsp finely chopped parsley
finely grated rind of ½ orange
salt and black pepper

NUTRITION NOTES

Per portion:
Energy	452Kcals/1902kJ
Fat	17.4g
Saturated fat	5.36g
Cholesterol	65.63mg
Fibre	2.56g

1 Cut the salmon into bite-sized pieces, arrange on a heatproof plate and cover with foil.

2 Bring a large pan of salted water to the boil, add the pasta and return to the boil. Place the plate of salmon on top and simmer for 10–12 minutes, until the pasta and salmon are cooked.

3 Drain the pasta and toss with the tomatoes and salmon. Mix together the crème fraîche, parsley, orange rind and pepper to taste, then toss into the salmon and pasta and serve hot or cold.

Stuffed Plaice Rolls

Plaice fillets are a good choice for families because they are economical, easy to cook and free of bones. If you prefer, the skin can be removed first.

Ingredients

Serves 4

1 medium courgette, grated
2 medium carrots, grated
*60ml/4 tbsp fresh wholemeal
   breadcrumbs*
15ml/1 tbsp lime or lemon juice
4 plaice fillets
salt and black pepper

1 Preheat the oven to 200°C/400°F/ Gas 6. Mix together the carrots and courgettes. Stir in the breadcrumbs, lime juice and seasoning.

2 Lay the fish fillets skin side up and divide the stuffing between them, spreading it evenly.

3 Roll up to enclose the stuffing and place in an ovenproof dish. Cover and bake for about 30 minutes, or until the fish flakes easily. Serve hot with new potatoes.

> **Cook's Tip**
> This recipe creates its own delicious juices, but for an extra sauce, stir chopped fresh parsley into a little low fat fromage frais and serve with the fish.

Nutrition Notes

Per portion:

Energy	158Kcals/665kJ
Fat	3.22g
Saturated fat	0.56g
Cholesterol	50.4mg
Fibre	1.94g

MACKEREL KEBABS WITH PARSLEY DRESSING

Oily fish such as mackerel are ideal for grilling as they cook quickly and need no extra oil.

INGREDIENTS

Serves 4

450g/1 lb mackerel fillets
finely grated rind and juice of 1 lemon
45ml/3 tbsp chopped fresh parsley
12 cherry tomatoes
8 pitted black olives
salt and black pepper

1 Cut the fish into 4cm/1½in chunks and place in a bowl with half the lemon rind and juice, half of the parsley and some seasoning. Cover the bowl and leave to marinate for 30 minutes.

2 Thread the chunks of fish on to eight long wooden or metal skewers, alternating them with the cherry tomatoes and olives. Cook the kebabs under a hot grill for 3–4 minutes, turning the kebabs occasionally, until the fish is cooked.

3 Mix the remaining lemon rind and juice with the remaining parsley in a small bowl, then season to taste with salt and pepper. Spoon the dressing over the kebabs and serve hot with plain boiled rice or noodles and a leafy green salad.

COOK'S TIP
When using wooden or bamboo kebab skewers, soak them first in a bowl of cold water for a few minutes to help prevent them burning.

NUTRITION NOTES

Per portion:

Energy	268Kcals/1126kJ
Fat	19.27g
Saturated fat	4.5g
Cholesterol	61.88mg
Fibre	1g

FISH FILLETS WITH A CHILLI SAUCE

Fish fillets, marinated with fresh coriander and lemon juice, then grilled and served with a chilli sauce, are delicious accompanied with saffron rice.

INGREDIENTS

Serves 4
4 flatfish fillets, such as plaice, sole or
  flounder, about 115g/4oz each
30ml/2 tbsp lemon juice
15ml/1 tbsp finely chopped fresh
  coriander
15ml/1 tbsp vegetable oil
lime wedges and coriander leaves, to
  garnish

For the sauce
5ml/1 tsp grated fresh root ginger
30ml/2 tbsp tomato purée
5ml/1 tsp sugar
5ml/1 tsp salt
15ml/1 tbsp chilli sauce
15ml/1 tbsp malt vinegar
300ml/½ pint/1¼ cups water

1 Rinse, pat dry and place the fish fillets in a medium bowl. Add the lemon juice, fresh coriander and oil and rub into the fish. Leave to marinate for at least 1 hour. The flavour will improve if you can leave it for longer.

2 To make the sauce, mix together all the sauce ingredients, pour into a small saucepan and simmer over a low heat for about 6 minutes, stirring occasionally.

3 Preheat the grill to medium. Cook the fillets under the grill for about 5–7 minutes.

4 When the fillets are cooked, remove and arrange them on a warmed serving dish.

5 The chilli sauce should now be fairly thick – about the consistency of a thick chicken soup.

6 Spoon the sauce over the fillets, garnish with the lime wedges and coriander leaves, and serve with rice.

NUTRITION NOTES

Per portion:
Energy	140Kcals/586kJ
Fat	5.28g
Saturated fat	0.78g
Cholesterol	47.25mg

STEAMING MUSSELS WITH A SPICY SAUCE

INGREDIENTS

Serves 4
75ml/5 tbsp red lentils
2 loaves French bread
1.75kg/4–4½ lb/4 pints live mussels
75ml/5 tbsp dry white wine

For the dipping sauce
30ml/2 tbsp sunflower oil
1 small onion, finely chopped
½ celery stick, finely chopped
1 large garlic clove, crushed
5ml/1 tsp medium-hot curry paste

1 Soak the lentils in a bowl filled with plenty of cold water until they are required. Preheat the oven to 150°C/300°F/Gas 2 and put the bread in to warm. Clean the mussels in plenty of cold water and pull off any stray beards. Discard any of the mussels that are damaged.

2 Place the mussels in a large saucepan or flameproof casserole. Add the white wine, cover and steam the mussels for about 8 minutes.

3 Transfer the mussels to a colander over a bowl to collect the juices. Keep warm until required.

4 For the dipping sauce, heat the sunflower oil in a second saucepan, add the onion and celery, and cook for about 3–4 minutes to soften without colouring. Strain the mussel juices into a measuring jug to remove any sand or grit. There will be approximately 400ml/14fl oz/1⅔ cups of liquid.

COOK'S TIP
Always buy mussels from a reputable supplier and ensure that the shells are tightly closed. Atlantic blue shell mussels are the most common. Small mussels are preferred for their sweet, tender flavour.

5 Add the mussel juices to the saucepan, then add the garlic, curry paste and lentils. Bring to the boil and simmer for a further 10–12 minutes or until the lentils have fallen apart.

6 Tip the mussels out on to four serving plates and serve with the dipping sauce, the warm French bread and a bowl to put the empty shells in.

NUTRITION NOTES
Per portion:	
Energy	627Kcals/2634kJ
Fat	12.68g
Saturated fat	2.24g
Cholesterol	135mg
Fibre	3.85g

OATY HERRINGS WITH RED SALSA

Herrings are one of the most economical and nutritious fish. If you buy them ready filletted, they're much easier to eat than the whole fish.

INGREDIENTS

Serves 4
30ml/2 tbsp skimmed milk
10ml/2 tsp Dijon mustard
2 large herrings, filletted
50g/2oz/⅔ cup rolled oats
salt and black pepper

For the salsa
1 small red pepper, seeded
4 medium tomatoes
1 spring onion, chopped
15ml/1 tbsp lime juice
5ml/1 tsp caster sugar

1 Preheat the oven to 200°C/400°F/ Gas 6. To make the salsa, place the pepper, tomatoes, spring onion, lime juice, sugar and seasoning in a food processor. Process until finely chopped.

2 Mix the milk and mustard, and the oats and pepper. Dip fillets into the mustard mixture, then oats to coat.

3 Place on a baking sheet, then bake for 20 minutes. Serve with the salsa.

NUTRITION NOTES
Per portion:

Energy	261Kcals/1097kJ
Fat	15.56g
Saturated fat	3.17g
Cholesterol	52.65mg
Fibre	2.21g

SPICED RAINBOW TROUT

Farmed rainbow trout are very good value and cook very quickly on a grill or barbecue. Herring and mackerel can be cooked in this way too.

INGREDIENTS

Serves 4
4 large rainbow trout fillets (about 150g/5oz each)
15ml/1 tbsp ground coriander
1 garlic clove, crushed
30ml/2 tbsp finely chopped fresh mint
5ml/1 tsp paprika
175g/6oz/¾ cup natural yogurt
salad and pitta bread, to serve

1 With a sharp knife, slash the flesh of the fish fillets through the skin fairly deeply at intervals.

2 Mix together the coriander, garlic, mint, paprika and yogurt. Spread this mixture evenly over the fish and leave to marinate for about an hour.

3 Cook the fish under a moderately hot grill or on a barbecue, turning occasionally, until crisp and golden. Serve hot with a crisp salad and some warmed pitta bread.

> COOK'S TIP
> If you are using the grill, it is best to line the grill pan with foil before cooking the trout.

NUTRITION NOTES
Per portion:

Energy	188Kcals/792kJ
Fat	5.66g
Saturated fat	1.45g
Cholesterol	110.87mg
Fibre	0.05g

HOKI BALLS IN TOMATO SAUCE

This quick meal is a good choice for young children, as you can guarantee no bones. If you like, add a dash of chilli sauce.

INGREDIENTS

Serves 4

450g/1 lb hoki or other white fish fillets, skinned
60ml/4 tbsp fresh wholemeal bread-crumbs
30ml/2 tbsp snipped chives or spring onion
400g/14oz can chopped tomatoes
50g/2oz/¾ cup button mushrooms, sliced
salt and black pepper

1 Cut the fish fillets into large chunks and place in a food processor. Add the wholemeal breadcrumbs, chives or spring onion. Season to taste with salt and pepper and process until the fish is finely chopped, but still has some texture left.

2 Divide the fish mixture into about 16 even-sized pieces, then mould them into balls with your hands.

3 Place the tomatoes and mushrooms in a wide saucepan and cook over a medium heat until boiling. Add the fish balls, cover and simmer for about 10 minutes, until cooked. Serve hot.

COOK'S TIP
Hoki is a good choice for this dish but if it's not available, use cod, haddock or whiting instead.

NUTRITION NOTES

Per portion:	
Energy	138Kcals/580kJ
Fat	1.38g
Saturated fat	0.24g
Cholesterol	51.75mg
Fibre	1.89g

TUNA AND CORN FISH CAKES

These economical little tuna fish cakes are quick to make. Either use fresh mashed potatoes, or make a storecupboard version with instant mash.

INGREDIENTS

Serves 4

300g/11oz/1¼ cups cooked mashed potatoes
200g/7oz can tuna fish in soya oil, drained
115g/4oz/¾ cup canned or frozen sweetcorn
30ml/2 tbsp chopped fresh parsley
50g/2oz/1 cup fresh white or brown breadcrumbs
salt and black pepper
lemon wedges, to serve

1 Place the mashed potato in a bowl and stir in the tuna fish, sweetcorn and chopped parsley.

2 Season to taste with salt and pepper, then shape into eight patty shapes with your hands.

3 Spread out the breadcrumbs on a plate and press the fish cakes into the breadcrumbs to coat lightly, then place on a baking sheet.

4 Cook the fish cakes under a moderately hot grill until crisp and golden brown, turning once. Serve hot with lemon wedges and fresh vegetables.

COOK'S TIP
For simple storecupboard variations which are just as nutritious, try using canned sardines, red or pink salmon, or smoked mackerel in place of the tuna.

NUTRITION NOTES

Per portion:

Energy	203Kcals/852kJ
Fat	4.62g
Saturated fat	0.81g
Cholesterol	21.25mg
Fibre	1.82g

FISH AND VEGETABLE KEBABS

Serves 4

275g/10oz cod fillets, or any other
  firm, white fish fillets
45ml/3 tbsp lemon juice
5ml/1 tsp grated fresh root ginger
2 green chillies, very finely chopped
15ml/1 tbsp very finely chopped fresh
  coriander
15ml/1 tbsp very finely chopped fresh
  mint
5ml/1 tsp ground coriander
5ml/1 tsp salt
1 red pepper
1 green pepper
½ cauliflower
8 button mushrooms
8 cherry tomatoes
15ml/1 tbsp soya oil
1 lime, quartered, to garnish

COOK'S TIP
Use different vegetables to the ones
suggested, if wished. Try baby corn
instead of mushrooms and broccoli
in place of the cauliflower.

1 Cut the fish fillets into large chunks
using a sharp knife.

2 In a large mixing bowl, blend
together the lemon juice, ginger,
chopped green chillies, fresh coriander,
mint, ground coriander and salt. Add
the fish chunks and leave to marinate
for about 30 minutes.

3 Cut the red and green peppers into
large squares and divide the cauliflower into individual florets.

4 Preheat the grill to hot. Arrange the
prepared vegetables alternately with
the fish pieces on four skewers.

5 Baste the kebabs with the oil and
any remaining marinade. Transfer
to a flameproof dish and grill for about
7–10 minutes or until the fish is cooked
right through. Garnish with the lime
quarters, and serve the kebabs either on
their own or with saffron rice.

NUTRITION NOTES	
Per portion:	
Energy	130Kcals/546kJ
Fat	4.34g
Saturated fat	0.51g
Cholesterol	32.54mg

GLAZED GARLIC PRAWNS

A fairly simple and quick dish to prepare, it is best to peel the prawns as this helps them to absorb maximum flavour. Serve as a main course with a variety of accompaniments, or with a salad as a starter.

INGREDIENTS

Serves 4
15ml/1 tbsp sunflower oil
3 garlic cloves, roughly chopped
3 tomatoes, chopped
2.5ml/½ tsp salt
5ml/1 tsp crushed dried red chillies
5ml/1 tsp lemon juice
15ml/1 tbsp mango chutney
1 green chilli, chopped
15–20 cooked king prawns, peeled
fresh coriander leaves and 2 chopped
  spring onions, to garnish

NUTRITION NOTES	
Per portion:	
Energy	90Kcals/380kJ
Fat	3.83g
Saturated fat	0.54g
Cholesterol	30.37mg

1 Heat the oil in a medium saucepan, and add the chopped garlic.

2 Lower the heat. Add the chopped tomatoes along with the salt, crushed chillies, lemon juice, mango chutney and chopped fresh chilli.

3 Finally add the prawns, turn up the heat and stir-fry quickly until they are heated through.

4 Transfer to a serving dish. Serve immediately garnished with fresh coriander leaves and chopped spring onions.

COD CREOLE

INGREDIENTS

Serves 4

450g/1 lb cod fillets, skinned
15ml/1 tbsp lime or lemon juice
10ml/2 tsp olive oil
1 medium onion, finely chopped
1 green pepper, seeded and sliced
2.5ml/½ tsp cayenne pepper
2.5ml/½ tsp garlic salt
400g/14oz can chopped tomatoes

NUTRITION NOTES

Per portion:

Energy	130Kcals/546kJ
Fat	2.61g
Saturated fat	0.38g
Cholesterol	51.75mg
Fibre	1.61g

1 Cut the cod fillets into bite-sized chunks and sprinkle with the lime or lemon juice.

2 In a large, non-stick pan, heat the olive oil and fry the onion and pepper gently until softened. Add the cayenne pepper and garlic salt.

3 Stir in the cod with the chopped tomatoes. Bring to the boil, then cover and simmer for about 5 minutes, or until the fish flakes easily. Serve with boiled rice or potatoes.

FIVE-SPICE FISH

Chinese mixtures of spicy, sweet and sour flavours are particularly successful with fish, and dinner is ready in minutes.

INGREDIENTS

Serves 4

4 white fish fillets, such as cod, haddock
or hoki (about 175g/6oz each)
5ml/1 tsp Chinese five-spice powder
20ml/4 tsp cornflour
15ml/1 tbsp sesame or sunflower oil
3 spring onions, shredded
5ml/1 tsp finely chopped root ginger
150g/5oz button mushrooms, sliced
115g/4oz baby corn cobs, sliced
30ml/2 tbsp soy sauce
45ml/3 tbsp dry sherry or apple juice
5ml/1 tsp sugar
salt and black pepper

1 Toss the fish in the five-spice powder and cornflour to coat.

2 Heat the oil in a frying pan or wok and stir-fry the onions, ginger mushrooms and corn cobs for about 1 minute. Add the fish and cook for 2–3 minutes, turning once.

3 Mix together the soy sauce, sherry and sugar then pour over the fish. Simmer for 2 minutes, adjust the seasoning, then serve with noodles and stir-fried vegetables.

NUTRITION NOTES

Per portion:

Energy	213Kcals/893kJ
Fat	4.41g
Saturated fat	0.67g
Cholesterol	80.5mg
Fibre	1.08g

Grilled Snapper with Mango Salsa

Serves 4

350g/12oz new potatoes

3 eggs

115g/4 oz green beans, topped, tailed and halved

4 red snapper, about 350g/12oz each, scaled and gutted

30ml/2 tbsp olive oil

175g/6oz mixed lettuce leaves

10 cherry tomatoes, to serve

salt and black pepper

For the salsa

45ml/3 tbsp chopped fresh coriander

1 ripe mango, peeled, stoned and diced

½ red chilli, seeded and chopped

2.5cm/1 in fresh root ginger, grated

juice of 2 limes

generous pinch of celery salt

NUTRITION NOTES

Per portion:

Energy	405Kcals/1702kJ
Fat	15.59g
Saturated fat	2.06g
Cholesterol	163.62mg
Fibre	2.03g

---

1 Place the potatoes in a large saucepan and cover with cold salted water. Bring to the boil and simmer for about 15–20 minutes. Drain and set aside.

2 Bring a second large pan of salted water to the boil. Put in the eggs and boil for 4 minutes.

3 Add the beans and cook for a further 6 minutes, so that the eggs have had a total of 10 minutes. Remove the eggs from the pan, cool, peel and cut into quarters. Drain the beans and set aside.

4 Preheat a moderate grill. Slash each snapper three times on either side, moisten with oil and cook for about 12 minutes, turning once.

5 For the dressing, place the coriander in a food processor or blender. Add the mango, chilli, ginger, lime juice and celery salt, and process until smooth.

6 Moisten the lettuce leaves with olive oil, and divide them among four large plates.

7 Arrange the snapper over the lettuce and season to taste. Halve the new potatoes and tomatoes, and distribute them with the beans and quartered hard-boiled eggs over the salad. Serve with the salsa dressing.

SALMON RISOTTO WITH CUCUMBER

Any rice can be used for risotto, although the creamiest ones are made with short grain arborio and carnaroli rice. Fresh tarragon and cucumber combine well to bring out the flavour of the salmon.

INGREDIENTS

Serves 4

25g/1oz/2 tbsp sunflower margarine
1 small bunch spring onions, white part
  only, chopped
½ cucumber, peeled, seeded and
  chopped
400g/14oz/1¼ cups short grain
  risotto rice
900ml/1½ pints/3¾ cups chicken or
  fish stock
150ml/¼ pint/⅔ cup dry white wine
450g/1 lb salmon fillet, skinned and
  diced

COOK'S TIP
Long grain rice can also be used for this recipe. Reduce the stock to 750ml/1¼ pints/3⅔ cups.

1 Heat the margarine in a large saucepan, and add the spring onions and cucumber. Cook for about 2–3 minutes without colouring.

2 Add the rice, stock and wine and return to the boil.

NUTRITION NOTES	
Per portion:	
Energy	653Kcals/2742kJ
Fat	19.88g
Saturated fat	6.99g
Cholesterol	70.63mg
Fibre	0.91g

3 Simmer the wine and stock mixture for about 10 minutes, stirring occasionally. Stir in the diced salmon and tarragon. Continue cooking for a further 5 minutes, then switch off the heat. Cover and leave to stand for 5 minutes before serving.

JAMAICAN COD STEAKS WITH RAGOUT

Spicy hot from Kingston town, this is a fast fish dish.

INGREDIENTS

Serves 4
finely grated zest of ½ orange
30ml/2 tbsp black peppercorns
15ml/1 tbsp allspice berries or
* Jamaican pepper*
2.5ml/½ tsp salt
4 cod fillet steaks, about 175g/6oz each
groundnut oil, for frying
new potatoes, to serve (optional)
45ml/3 tbsp chopped fresh parsley,
* to garnish*

For the ragout
30ml/2 tbsp groundnut oil
1 medium onion, chopped
2.5cm/1 in piece fresh root ginger,
* peeled and grated*
450g/1 lb fresh pumpkin, peeled,
* deseeded and chopped*
3–4 shakes of Tabasco sauce
30ml/2 tbsp soft brown sugar
15ml/1 tbsp vinegar

1 For the ragout, heat the oil in a heavy saucepan and add the onion and ginger. Cover and cook, stirring, for 3–4 minutes until soft.

2 Add the chopped pumpkin, Tabasco sauce, brown sugar and vinegar, cover and cook over a low heat for about 10–12 minutes until softened.

3 Combine the orange zest, peppercorns, allspice or Jamaican pepper and salt, then crush coarsely using a pestle and mortar. (Alternatively, coarsely grind the peppercorns in a pepper mill and combine with the zest and seasoning.)

4 Sprinkle the spice mixture over both sides of the fish and moisten with a little oil.

5 Heat a large frying pan and dry-fry the cod steaks for about 12 minutes, turning once.

6 Serve the cod steaks with a spoonful of pumpkin ragout and new potatoes, if required, and garnish the ragout with chopped fresh parsley.

NUTRITION NOTES

Per portion:	
Energy	324Kcals/1360kJ
Fat	14.9g
Saturated fat	2.75g
Cholesterol	80.5mg
Fibre	1.92g

COOK'S TIP
This recipe can be adapted using any types of firm pink or white fish that is available, such as haddock, whiting, monkfish, halibut or tuna.

TUNA FISH AND FLAGEOLET BEAN SALAD

Two cans of tuna fish form the basis of this delicious and easy-to-make storecupboard salad.

INGREDIENTS

Serves 4

90ml/6 tbsp reduced calorie mayonnaise
5ml/1 tsp mustard
30ml/2 tbsp capers
45ml/3 tbsp chopped fresh parsley
pinch of celery salt
2 x 200g/7oz cans tuna fish in brine, drained
3 little gem lettuces
400g/14oz can flageolet beans, drained
12 cherry tomatoes, halved
400g/14oz can baby artichoke hearts, halved
toasted sesame bread or sticks, to serve

NUTRITION NOTES

Per portion:

Energy	299Kcals/1255kJ
Fat	13.91g
Saturated fat	2.12g
Cholesterol	33mg
Fibre	6.36g

1 Combine the mayonnaise, mustard, capers and parsley in a mixing bowl. Season to taste with celery salt.

2 Flake the tuna into the dressing and toss gently.

3 Arrange the lettuce leaves on four plates, then spoon the tuna mixture on to the leaves.

COOK'S TIP
If flageolet beans are not available, use cannellini beans.

4 Spoon the flageolet beans to one side, followed by the tomatoes and artichoke hearts.

5 Serve with slices of toasted sesame bread or sticks.

PASTA, PIZZAS, PULSES AND GRAINS

Pasta, pizzas, pulses and grain dishes should be encouraged at family meals as they're mostly very healthy foods. Pasta and rice contain good amounts of protein, carbohydrate and vitamins, are particularly low in fat, and are also extremely versatile.

Add variety to meals by introducing different grains, such as polenta, couscous or bulgur wheat, which are just as easy and healthy as rice, but will help to keep appetites lively.

Penne and Aubergine with Mint Pesto

This splendid variation on the classic Italian pesto uses fresh mint rather than basil.

INGREDIENTS

Serves 4
2 large aubergines
pinch of salt
450g/1 lb/5 cups penne
50g/2oz/½ cup walnut halves

For the pesto
25g/1oz/1 cup fresh mint
15g/½oz/½ cup flat leaf parsley
40g/1½oz/½ cup walnuts
40g/1½oz/½ cup Parmesan cheese,
   finely grated
2 garlic cloves
45ml/3 tbsp olive oil
salt and black pepper

NUTRITION NOTES

Per portion:	
Energy	777Kcals/2364kJ
Fat	38.11g
Saturated fat	6.29g
Cholesterol	10mg
Fibre	8.57g

1 Cut the aubergines lengthways into 1cm/½ in slices.

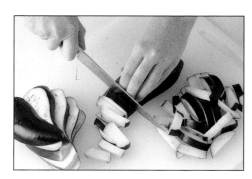

2 Cut the slices again crossways to give short strips.

3 Layer the strips in a colander with salt and leave to stand for 30 minutes over a plate to catch any juices. Rinse well in cool water and drain.

4 For the pesto, place all the ingredients, except the oil, in a food processor or blender and blend until smooth, then gradually add the oil in a thin stream until the mixture amalgamates. Season to taste.

5 Bring a large saucepan of water to the boil, toss in the penne and cook for 8 minutes or until nearly cooked. Add the aubergine and cook for a further 3 minutes.

6 Drain well and mix in half of the mint pesto and walnut halves. Serve with the remaining pesto and walnut halves on top.

TAGLIATELLE WITH PEA AND BEAN SAUCE

A creamy pea sauce makes a wonderful combination with the crunchy young vegetables.

INGREDIENTS

Serves 4

15ml/1 tbsp olive oil
1 garlic clove, crushed
6 spring onions, sliced
115g/4oz/1 cup fresh or frozen baby
    peas, defrosted
350g/12oz fresh young asparagus
30ml/2 tbsp chopped fresh sage, plus
    extra leaves, to garnish
finely grated rind of 2 lemons
400ml/14fl oz/1⅔ cups vegetable stock
    or water
225g/8oz/1½ cups fresh or frozen
    broad beans, defrosted
450g/1 lb tagliatelle
60ml/4 tbsp low fat natural yogurt

NUTRITION NOTES

Per portion:

Energy	509 Kcals/2139kJ
Fat	6.75g
Saturated fat	0.95g
Cholesterol	0.6mg
Fibre	9.75g

1 Heat the oil in a pan. Add the garlic and spring onions, and cook gently for about 2–3 minutes until softened.

3 Meanwhile remove the outer skins from the broad beans and discard.

5 Cook the tagliatelle following the manufacturer's instructions until *al dente*. Drain well.

6 Add the cooked asparagus and shelled beans to the sauce, and reheat. Stir in the yogurt and toss into the tagliatelle. Garnish with a few extra sage leaves, and serve immediately.

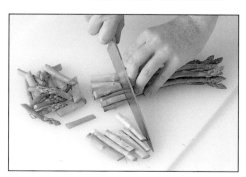

2 Add the peas and a third of the asparagus, together with the sage, lemon rind and stock or water. Simmer for about 10 minutes. Process in a food processor or blender until smooth.

4 Cut the remaining asparagus into 5cm/2 in lengths, trimming off any tough fibrous stems, and blanch in boiling water for about 2 minutes.

COOK'S TIP
Frozen peas and beans have been suggested as an option here to cut down the preparation time, but the dish tastes even better if you use fresh young vegetables when in season.

SPAGHETTI WITH HERB SAUCE

Serves 4

50g/2oz/2 cups chopped fresh mixed
  herbs, such as parsley, basil and thyme
2 garlic cloves, crushed
60ml/4 tbsp pine nuts, toasted
60ml/4 tbsp olive oil
350g/12oz dried spaghetti
60ml/4 tbsp grated Parmesan cheese
salt and black pepper
basil leaves, to garnish

COOK'S TIP
Spaghetti should be cooked until
it is just firm to the bite, or *al
dente*. If it is allowed to cook for
too long, it will become soggy.

1 Put the herbs, garlic and half the
pine nuts into a food processor or
blender. With the machine running,
gradually add the oil and process to
form a thick purée.

2 Cook the spaghetti in plenty of
boiling salted water for about
8 minutes until *al dente*. Drain.

NUTRITION NOTES	
Per portion:	
Energy	694Kcals/2915kJ
Fat	42.01g
Saturated fat	6.80g
Cholesterol	7.50mg
Fibre	3.18g

3 Transfer the herb purée to a large
warm bowl, then add the spaghetti
and Parmesan. Toss well to coat the
pasta with the sauce. Sprinkle over the
remaining pine nuts and the basil
leaves, and serve immediately.

CHIVE OMELETTE STIR-FRY

Serves 3–4

2 eggs
15–30ml/1–2 tbsp snipped fresh chives
30ml/2 tbsp groundnut oil
1 garlic clove, chopped
1cm/½ in piece fresh root ginger,
  chopped
2 celery sticks, cut into shreds
2 carrots, cut into shreds
2 small courgettes, cut into shreds
4 spring onions, cut into shreds
1 bunch radishes, sliced
115g/4oz/1⅓ cup beansprouts
¼ head of Chinese leaves, shredded
15ml/1 tbsp sesame oil
salt and black pepper

NUTRITION NOTES	
Per portion:	
Energy	188Kcals/788kJ
Fat	13.3g
Saturated fat	2.76g
Cholesterol	146.3mg
Fibre	3.85g

1 Whisk together the eggs, chives and
seasoning in a bowl. Heat about
5ml/1 tsp of the groundnut oil in an
omelette pan and pour in just enough
of the egg mixture to cover the base of
the pan. Cook for about 1 minute until
set, then turn over the omelette and
cook for a further minute.

2 Tip out the omelette on to a plate
and cook the rest of the egg mixture
in the same way to make several
omelettes, adding extra oil to the pan,
if neccessary. Roll up each omelette and
slice thinly. Keep the omelettes warm in
a low oven until required.

3 Heat the remaining oil in a wok or
large frying pan, add the chopped
garlic and ginger and stir-fry for a few
seconds to flavour the oil.

4 Add the shredded celery, carrots
and courgettes and stir-fry the
vegetables for about 1 minute. Add the
radishes, beansprouts, spring onions
and Chinese leaves and stir-fry for a
further 2–3 minutes, until all the vegetables are tender but still crunchy.
Sprinkle a little sesame oil over the
vegetables and toss gently.

5 Serve the stir-fried vegetables at
once with the sliced chive omelettes
scattered over the top.

TABBOULEH WITH FENNEL

A fresh salad originating in the Middle East that is perfect for a summer lunch. Serve with lettuce and pitta bread.

INGREDIENTS

Serves 4
225g/8oz/1¼ cups bulgur wheat
2 fennel bulbs
1 small red chilli, seeded and chopped
1 celery stick, finely sliced
30ml/2 tbsp olive oil
finely grated rind and juice of
   2 lemons
6–8 spring onions, chopped
90ml/6 tbsp chopped fresh mint
90ml/6 tbsp chopped fresh parsley
1 pomegranate, seeded
salt and black pepper

NUTRITION NOTES

Per portion:
Energy	188Kcals/791kJ
Fat	4.67g
Saturated fat	0.62g
Cholesterol	0
Fibre	2.17g

1 Place the bulgur wheat in a bowl and pour over enough cold water to cover. Leave to stand for 30 minutes.

3 Halve the fennel bulbs and carefully cut into very fine slices with a sharp knife.

2 Drain the wheat through a sieve, pressing out any excess water using a spoon.

4 Mix all the remaining ingredients together, including the soaked bulgur wheat and fennel. Season well, cover, and set aside for 30 minutes before serving.

COOK'S TIP
Fennel has a very distinctive aniseed flavour. When you are buying fennel, choose well-rounded bulbs which are pale green to white in colour. Avoid any that are deep green. Fennel never goes out of season, it is available all year round.

Sweet Vegetable Couscous

A wonderful combination of sweet vegetables and spices, this makes a substantial winter dish.

INGREDIENTS

Serves 4–6
generous pinch of saffron threads
45ml/3 tbsp boiling water
15ml/1 tbsp olive oil
1 red onion, sliced
2 garlic cloves
1–2 red chillies, seeded and finely chopped
2.5ml/½ tsp ground ginger
2.5ml/½ tsp ground cinnamon
400g/14oz can chopped tomatoes
300ml/½ pint/1¼ cups fresh vegetable stock or water
4 carrots, peeled and cut into 5mm/¼ in slices
2 turnips, peeled and cut into 2cm/¾ in cubes
450g/1 lb sweet potatoes, peeled and cut into 2cm/¾ in cubes
75g/3oz/⅓ cup raisins
2 courgettes, cut into 5mm/¼ in slices
400g/14oz can chick-peas, drained and rinsed
45ml/3 tbsp chopped fresh parsley
45ml/3 tbsp chopped fresh coriander
450g/1 lb/4 cups quick-cook couscous

1 Leave the saffron to infuse in the boiling water.

2 Heat the oil in a large saucepan or flameproof casserole. Add the onion, garlic and chillies, and cook gently for about 5 minutes.

3 Add the ground ginger and cinnamon, and gently cook for a further 1–2 minutes.

4 Add the tomatoes, stock or water, saffron and liquid, carrots, turnips, sweet potatoes and raisins, cover and simmer for a further 25 minutes.

5 Add the courgettes, chick-peas, parsley and coriander, and cook for a further 10 minutes.

6 Meanwhile prepare the couscous following the manufacturer's instructions, and then serve with the prepared vegetables.

NUTRITION NOTES

Per portion:
Energy	570Kcals/2393kJ
Fat	7.02g
Saturated fat	0.83g
Cholesterol	0
Fibre	10.04g

COOK'S TIP
Vegetable stock can be made from a variety of uncooked vegetables. These can include the outer leaves of cabbage, lettuce and other greens, carrot peelings, leeks and parsnips.

PASTA WITH PASSATA AND CHICK PEAS

INGREDIENTS

Serves 4
300g/10oz/2 cups pasta
5ml/1 tsp olive oil
1 small onion, finely chopped
1 garlic clove, crushed
1 celery stick, finely chopped
425g/15oz can chick-peas, drained
250ml/8 fl oz/1 cup passata
salt and black pepper
chopped fresh parsley, to garnish

1 Heat the olive oil in a non-stick pan and fry the onion, garlic and celery until softened but not browned. Stir in the chick-peas and passata, then cover and simmer for about 15 minutes.

2 Cook the pasta in a large pan of boiling, lightly salted water until just tender. Drain the pasta and toss into the sauce, then season to taste with salt and pepper. Sprinkle with chopped fresh parsley, then serve hot.

NUTRITION NOTES

Per portion:
Energy	374Kcals/1570kJ
Fat	4.44g
Saturated fat	0.32g
Cholesterol	0
Fibre	6.41g

PEPERONATA PIZZA

INGREDIENTS

Makes 2 large pizzas
450g/1 lb/4 cups plain flour
pinch of salt
1 sachet easy-blend yeast
about 350ml/12 fl oz/1½ cups warm water

For the topping
1 onion, sliced
10ml/2 tsp olive oil
2 large red and 2 yellow peppers, seeded and sliced
1 garlic clove, crushed
400g/14oz can tomatoes
8 pitted black olives, halved
salt and black pepper

NUTRITION NOTES

Per portion:
Energy	965Kcals/4052kJ
Fat	9.04g
Saturated fat	1.07g
Cholesterol	0
Fibre	14.51g

1 To make the dough, sift the flour and salt into a bowl and stir in the yeast. Stir in just enough warm water to mix to a soft dough.

2 Knead for 5 minutes until smooth. Cover and leave in a warm place for about 1 hour, or until doubled in size.

3 To make the topping, fry the onion in the oil until soft, then stir in the peppers, garlic and tomatoes. Cover and simmer for 30 minutes, until no free liquid remains. Season to taste.

4 Preheat the oven to 230°C/450°F/ Gas 8. Divide the dough in half and press out each piece on a lightly oiled baking sheet to a 28cm/11in round, turning up the edges slightly.

5 Spread over the topping, dot with olives and bake for 15–20 minutes. Serve hot or cold with salad.

CAMPANELLE WITH YELLOW PEPPER SAUCE

Roasted yellow peppers make a deliciously sweet and creamy sauce to serve with pasta.

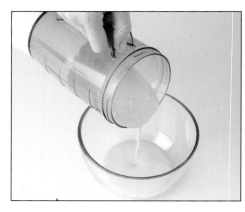

INGREDIENTS

Serves 4
2 yellow peppers, halved
50g/2oz/¼ cup low fat soft goat's cheese
115g/4oz/½ cup low fat fromage blanc
salt and black pepper
450g/1 lb/5 cups campanelle pasta
50g/2oz/¼ cup flaked almonds, toasted, to serve

NUTRITION NOTES

Per portion:
Energy	529Kcals/2221kJ
Fat	11.18 g
Saturated fat	0.88g
Cholesterol	9.04mg
Fibre	5.69g

1 Preheat the grill. Place the yellow pepper halves under the grill until charred and blistered. Place in a plastic bag to cool. Peel and remove the seeds.

> **COOK'S TIP**
> Always cut the stalk ends from peppers and discard the mid-ribs and seeds.

2 Place the pepper flesh in a food processor or blender with the goat's cheese and fromage blanc. Process until smooth. Season with salt and lots of black pepper.

3 Cook the pasta following the manufacturer's instructions until *al dente*. Drain well.

4 Toss with the sauce and serve the dish sprinkled with the toasted flaked almonds.

GREEN LENTIL AND CABBAGE SALAD

This warm crunchy salad makes a satisfying meal if served with crusty French bread or whole-meal rolls.

— INGREDIENTS —

Serves 4–6

225g/8oz/1¼ cups puy lentils
1.3 litres/2¼ pints/6 cups cold water
1 garlic clove
1 bay leaf
1 onion, peeled and studded with 2 cloves
15ml/1 tbsp olive oil
1 red onion, finely sliced
2 garlic cloves, crushed
15ml/1 tbsp thyme leaves
350g/12oz/3¼ cups cabbage, finely shredded
finely grated rind and juice of 1 lemon
15ml/1 tbsp raspberry vinegar
salt and black pepper

— NUTRITION NOTES —

Per portion:

Energy	228Kcals/959kJ
Fat	4.38g
Saturated fat	0.44g
Cholesterol	0
Fibre	8.09g

1 Rinse the lentils in cold water and place in a large pan with the water, peeled garlic clove, bay leaf and clove-studded onion. Bring to the boil and cook for about 10 minutes. Reduce the heat, cover the pan, and simmer gently for a further 15–20 minutes. Drain and remove the onion, garlic and bay leaf.

2 Heat the oil in a large pan. Add the red onion, garlic and thyme, and cook for 5 minutes until softened.

3 Add the cabbage and cook for a further 3–5 minutes until just cooked but still crunchy (*al dente*).

4 Stir in the cooked lentils, lemon rind and juice and the raspberry vinegar. Season to taste and serve.

COOK'S TIP
There are several varieties of cabbage available such as spring, summer, winter, white and red cabbage. White cabbage is excellent in salads, choose one with a firm, compact head and avoid those with loose curling leaves.

LEMON AND GINGER SPICY BEANS

INGREDIENTS

Serves 4

30ml/2 tbsp roughly chopped fresh
   root ginger
3 garlic cloves, roughly chopped
250ml/8fl oz/1 cup cold water
15ml/1 tbsp sunflower oil
1 large onion, thinly sliced
1 red chilli, seeded and finely
   chopped
1.5ml/¼ tsp cayenne pepper
10ml/2 tsp ground cumin
5ml/1 tsp ground coriander
2.5ml/½ tsp ground turmeric
30ml/2 tbsp lemon juice
75g/3oz/3 cups chopped fresh
   coriander
400g/14oz can black-eyed beans,
   drained and rinsed
400g/14oz can aduki beans,
   drained and rinsed
400g/14oz can haricot beans,
   drained and rinsed
salt and black pepper
crusty bread, to serve

1 Place the ginger, garlic and
60ml/4 tbsp of the cold water in a
food processor or blender and process
until smooth.

2 Heat the oil in a saucepan. Add the
onion and chilli, and cook gently
for about 5 minutes until softened.

3 Add the cayenne pepper, cumin,
ground coriander and turmeric, and
stir-fry for a further 1 minute.

4 Stir in the ginger and garlic paste
from the food processor or blender
and cook for a further minute.

5 Add the remaining water, lemon
juice and fresh coriander, stir well
and bring to the boil. Cover the pan
tightly and cook for about 5 minutes.

6 Add all the beans and cook for a
further 5–10 minutes. Season with
salt and pepper, to taste, and serve with
crusty bread.

NUTRITION NOTES	
Per portion:	
Energy	281Kcals/1180kJ
Fat	4.3g
Saturated fat	0.42g
Cholesterol	0
Fibre	10.76g

SESAME NOODLE SALAD WITH PEANUTS

An Orient-inspired salad with crunchy vegetables and a light soy dressing. The hot peanuts make a surprisingly successful union with the cold noodles.

INGREDIENTS

Serves 4

350g/12oz egg noodles
2 carrots, peeled and cut into fine
　julienne strips
½ cucumber, peeled and cut into
　1cm/½ in cubes
115g/4oz celeriac, peeled and cut into
　fine julienne strips
6 spring onions, finely sliced
8 canned water chestnuts, drained and
　finely sliced
175g/6oz/2 cups beansprouts
1 small green chilli, chopped, plus
　1 green chilli, to garnish
30ml/2 tbsp sesame seeds and
　115g/4oz/1 cup peanuts, to serve

For the dressing

15ml/1 tbsp dark soy sauce
15ml/1 tbsp light soy sauce
15ml/1 tbsp clear honey
15ml/1 tbsp rice wine or dry sherry
15ml/1 tbsp sesame oil

3 Mix the noodles with all of the prepared vegetables.

5 Place the sesame seeds and peanuts on separate baking trays and bake for 5 minutes. Remove the sesame seeds and continue to cook the peanuts for 5 minutes more, or until browned.

6 Sprinkle the sesame seeds and peanuts over each portion and serve at once, garnished with chillies.

1 Preheat the oven to 200°C/400°F/ Gas 6. Bring a large saucepan of water to the boil, toss in the egg noodles and cook according to the manufacturer's instructions.

2 Drain the noodles, refresh in cold water, then drain again.

4 For the dressing, combine the ingredients in a bowl, then toss into the vegetable mixture. Divide the salad among four plates.

NUTRITION NOTES	
Per portion:	
Energy	634Kcals/2664kJ
Fat	28.1g
Saturated fat	4.03g
Cholesterol	0
Fibre	5.33g

PENNE WITH BROCCOLI AND CHILLI

INGREDIENTS

Serves 4
450g/1 lb small broccoli florets
30ml/2 tbsp stock
1 garlic clove, crushed
1 small red chilli pepper, sliced, or
*   2.5ml/½ tsp chilli sauce*
60ml/4 tbsp natural low fat yogurt
30ml/2 tbsp toasted pine nuts or
*   cashews*
350g/12oz/3¾ cups penne pasta
salt and black pepper

2 Heat the stock and add the crushed garlic and chilli or chilli sauce. Stir over a low heat for 2–3 minutes.

1 Add the pasta to a large pan of lightly salted boiling water and return to the boil. Place the broccoli in a steamer basket over the top. Cover and cook for 8–10 minutes until both are just tender. Drain.

3 Stir in the broccoli, pasta and yogurt. Adjust the seasoning, sprinkle with nuts and serve hot.

NUTRITION NOTES

Per portion:
Energy	403Kcals/1695kJ
Fat	7.87g
Saturated fat	0.89g
Cholesterol	0.6mg
Fibre	5.83g

CREOLE JAMBALAYA

INGREDIENTS

Serves 6
4 boneless chicken thighs, skinned and
*   diced*
1 large green pepper, seeded and sliced
3 celery sticks, sliced
4 spring onions, sliced
about 300ml/½ pint/1¼ cups chicken
*   stock*
400g/14oz can tomatoes
5ml/1 tsp ground cumin
5ml/1 tsp ground allspice
2.5ml/½ tsp cayenne pepper
5ml/1 tsp dried thyme
300g/10oz/1½ cups long grain rice
200g/7oz cooked, peeled prawns
salt and black pepper

2 Add the pepper, celery and onions with 15ml/1 tbsp stock. Cook for a few minutes to soften, then add the tomatoes, spices and thyme.

1 Fry the chicken in a non-stick pan without fat, turning occasionally, until golden brown.

3 Stir in the rice and stock. Cover closely and cook for about 20 minutes, stirring occasionally, until the rice is tender. Add more stock if necessary.

4 Add the prawns and heat well. Season and serve with a crisp salad.

NUTRITION NOTES

Per portion:
Energy	282Kcals/1185kJ
Fat	3.37g
Saturated fat	0.85g
Cholesterol	51.33mg
Fibre	1.55g

Thai Fragrant Rice

A lovely, soft, fluffy rice dish, perfumed with delicious and fresh lemon grass.

INGREDIENTS

Serves 4

1 piece lemon grass
2 limes
225g/8oz/1⅓ cups brown basmati rice
15ml/1 tbsp olive oil
1 onion, chopped
*2.5cm/1 in piece fresh root ginger,
   peeled and finely chopped*
7.5ml/1½ tsp coriander seeds
7.5ml/1½ tsp cumin seeds
*750ml/1¼ pints/3⅔ cups vegetable
   stock*
60ml/4 tbsp chopped fresh coriander
lime wedges, to serve

COOK'S TIP
Other varieties of rice, such as white basmati or long grain, can be used for this dish but you will need to adjust the cooking times as necessary.

1 Finely chop the lemon grass and remove the zest from the limes.

2 Rinse the rice in cold water. Drain through a sieve.

3 Heat the oil in a large saucepan and add the onion and spices and cook gently for about 2–3 minutes.

4 Add the rice and cook for a further minute, then add the stock or water and bring to the boil. Reduce the heat to very low and cover the pan. Cook gently for about 30 minutes then check the rice. If it is still crunchy, cover the pan again with the lid and leave for a further 3–5 minutes. Remove from the heat.

5 Stir in the fresh coriander, fluff up the grains, cover and leave for 10 minutes. Serve with lime wedges.

NUTRITION NOTES	
Per portion:	
Energy	259Kcals/1087kJ
Fat	5.27g
Saturated fat	0.81g
Cholesterol	0
Fibre	1.49g

PUMPKIN AND PISTACHIO RISOTTO

This elegant combination of creamy golden rice and orange pumpkin can be made as pale or bright as you like – simply add different quantities of saffron.

INGREDIENTS

Serves 4

1.2 litres/2 pints/5 cups vegetable stock or water
generous pinch of saffron threads
30ml/2 tbsp olive oil
1 onion, chopped
2 garlic cloves, crushed
900g/2 lb pumpkin, peeled, seeded and cut into 2cm/³⁄₄ in cubes
450g/1 lb/2 cups arborio rice
200ml/7fl oz/⁷⁄₈ cup dry white wine
15ml/1 tbsp Parmesan cheese, finely grated
50g/2oz/¹⁄₂cup pistachios
45ml/3 tbsp chopped fresh marjoram or oregano, plus extra leaves, to garnish
salt, freshly grated nutmeg and black pepper

NUTRITION NOTES

Per portion:
Energy	630Kcals/2646kJ
Fat	15.24g
Saturated fat	2.66g
Cholesterol	3.75mg
Fibre	2.59g

2 Heat the oil in a saucepan or flame-proof casserole. Add the onion and garlic, and cook gently for 5 minutes until softened. Add the pumpkin and rice and cook for a few more minutes until the rice looks transparent.

3 Pour in the wine and allow it to boil hard. When it is absorbed add a quarter of the stock or water and the infused saffron and liquid. Stir constantly until all the liquid is absorbed.

5 Cook the rice for about 25–30 minutes or until *al dente*. Stir in the Parmesan cheese, cover the pan and leave to stand for 5 minutes.

6 To finish, stir in the pistachios and marjoram or oregano. Season to taste with a little salt, nutmeg and pepper, and sprinkle over a few extra marjoram or oregano leaves.

1 Bring the stock or water to the boil and reduce to a low simmer. Ladle a little liquid into a small bowl. Add the saffron threads and leave to infuse.

4 Gradually add a ladleful of stock or water at a time, allowing the rice to absorb the liquid before adding more and stir constantly.

COOK'S TIP
Italian arborio rice is a special short grain rice that gives an authentic creamy consistency.

Tomato Rice

This dish is delicious and is substantial enough to be eaten as a complete meal on its own.

Ingredients

Serves 4
30ml/2 tbsp corn oil
2.5ml/½ tsp onion seeds
1 onion, sliced
2 tomatoes, sliced
1 orange or yellow pepper, chopped
5ml/1 tsp grated fresh root ginger
1 garlic clove, crushed
5ml/1 tsp chilli powder
30ml/2 tbsp chopped fresh coriander
1 potato, diced
7.5ml/1½ tsp salt
50g/2oz/½ cup frozen peas
400g/14oz/2 cups basmati rice, washed
700ml/24fl oz/3 cups water

Nutrition Notes	
Per portion:	
Energy	351Kcals/1475kJ
Fat	6.48g
Saturated fat	0.86g
Cholesterol	0

1 Heat the oil and fry the onion seeds for about 30 seconds. Add the sliced onion and fry for about 5 minutes.

2 Add the next nine ingredients and stir-fry over a medium heat for a further 5 minutes.

3 Add the rice and stir-fry for about 1 minute.

4 Pour in the water and bring to the boil, then lower the heat to medium. Cover and cook for a further 12–15 minutes. Leave the rice to stand for 5 minutes and serve.

Pea and Mushroom Pullao

It is best to use button mushrooms and petit pois for this delectable rice dish, as they make the pullao look very attractive and appetizing.

Ingredients

Serves 6
450g/1 lb/2¼ cups basmati rice
30ml/2 tbsp vegetable oil
2.5ml/½ tsp black cumin seeds
2 black cardamom pods
2 cinnamon sticks
3 garlic cloves, sliced
5ml/1 tsp salt
1 tomato, sliced
50g/2oz/⅔ cup button mushrooms
75g/3oz/⅓ heaped cup petit pois
750ml/1¼ pints/3⅔ cups water

Nutrition Notes	
Per portion:	
Energy	297Kcals/1246kJ
Fat	4.34g
Saturated fat	0.49g
Cholesterol	0

1 Wash the rice at least twice and set aside in a sieve.

2 Heat the oil in a medium saucepan and add the spices, garlic and salt.

3 Add the sliced tomato and button mushrooms, and stir-fry for about 2–3 minutes.

4 Add the rice and peas, and gently stir around making sure you do not break the rice.

5 Add the water and bring the mixture to the boil. Lower the heat, cover, and continue to cook for a further 15–20 minutes.

SPINACH AND HAZELNUT LASAGNE

A vegetarian dish which is hearty enough to satisfy meat-eaters too. Use frozen spinach if you're short of time.

INGREDIENTS

Serves 4

900g/2 lb fresh spinach
300ml/½ pint/1¼ cups vegetable or
    chicken stock
1 medium onion, finely chopped
1 garlic clove, crushed
75g/3oz/¾ cup hazelnuts
30ml/2 tbsp chopped fresh basil
6 sheets lasagne
400g/14oz can chopped tomatoes
200g/7oz/1 cup low fat fromage frais
flaked hazelnuts and chopped parsley,
    to garnish

1 Preheat the oven to 200°C/400°F/ Gas 6. Wash the spinach and place in a pan with just the water that clings to the leaves. Cook the spinach on a fairly high heat for 2 minutes until wilted. Drain well.

2 Heat 30ml/2 tbsp of the stock in a large pan and simmer the onion and garlic until soft. Stir in the spinach, hazelnuts and basil.

3 In a large ovenproof dish, layer the spinach, lasagne and tomatoes. Season well between the layers. Pour over the remaining stock. Spread the fromage frais over the top.

4 Bake the lasagne for about 45 minutes, or until golden brown. Serve hot, sprinkled with lines of flaked hazelnuts and chopped parsley.

> COOK'S TIP
> The flavour of hazelnuts is improved by roasting. Place them on a baking sheet and bake in a moderate oven, or under a hot grill, until light golden.

NUTRITION NOTES

Per portion:

Energy	365Kcals/1532kJ
Fat	17g
Saturated fat	1.46g
Cholesterol	0.5mg
Fibre	8.16g

CALZONE

Makes 4

450g/1 lb/4 cups plain flour
pinch of salt
1 sachet easy-blend yeast
about 350ml/12 fl oz/1½ cups warm
    water

For the filling

5ml/1 tsp olive oil
1 medium red onion, thinly sliced
3 medium courgettes, about 350g/12oz
    total weight, sliced
2 large tomatoes, diced
150g/5oz mozzarella cheese, diced
15ml/1 tbsp chopped fresh oregano
skimmed milk, to glaze
salt and black pepper

1 To make the dough, sift the flour and salt into a bowl and stir in the yeast. Stir in just enough warm water to mix to a soft dough.

2 Knead for 5 minutes until smooth. Cover and leave in a warm place for about 1 hour, or until doubled in size.

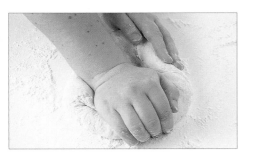

3 Meanwhile, to make the filling, heat the oil and sauté the onion and courgettes for 3–4 minutes. Remove from the heat and add the tomatoes, cheese, oregano and seasoning.

4 Preheat the oven to 220°C/425°F/ Gas 7. Knead the dough lightly and divide into four. Roll out each piece on a lightly floured surface to a 20cm/8in round and place a quarter of the filling on one half.

5 Brush the edges with milk and fold over to enclose the filling. Press firmly to enclose. Brush with milk.

6 Bake on an oiled baking sheet for 15–20 minutes. Serve hot or cold.

NUTRITION NOTES	
Per portion:	
Energy	544Kcals/2285kJ
Fat	10.93g
Saturated fat	5.49g
Cholesterol	24.42mg
Fibre	5.09g

TAGLIATELLE WITH HAZELNUT PESTO

Hazelnuts are lower in fat than other nuts, which makes them useful for this reduced-fat alternative to pesto sauce.

INGREDIENTS

Serves 4

2 garlic cloves, crushed
25g/1oz/1 cup fresh basil leaves
25g/1oz/¼ cup hazelnuts
200g/7oz/⅞ cup skimmed milk soft cheese
225g/8oz dried tagliatelle, or 450g/1 lb fresh
salt and black pepper

1 Place the garlic, basil, hazelnuts and cheese in a food processor or blender and process to a thick paste.

2 Cook the tagliatelle in lightly salted boiling water until just tender, then drain well.

3 Spoon the sauce into the hot pasta, tossing until melted. Sprinkle with pepper and serve hot.

NUTRITION NOTES

Per portion:

Energy	274Kcals/1155kJ
Fat	5.05g
Saturated fat	0.43g
Cholesterol	0.5mg
Fibre	2.14g

SPAGHETTI WITH TUNA SAUCE

A speedy midweek meal, which can also be made with other pasta shapes.

INGREDIENTS

Serves 4

225g/8oz dried spaghetti, or 450g/1 lb fresh
1 garlic clove, crushed
400g/14oz can chopped tomatoes
425g/15oz can tuna fish in brine, flaked
2.5ml/½ tsp chilli sauce (optional)
4 pitted black olives, chopped
salt and black pepper

> **COOK'S TIP**
> If fresh tuna is available, use 450g/1lb, cut into small chunks, and add after step 2. Simmer for 6–8 minutes, then add the chilli, olives and pasta.

1 Cook the spaghetti in lightly salted boiling water for 12 minutes or until just tender. Drain well and keep hot.

2 Add the garlic and tomatoes to the saucepan and bring to the boil. Simmer, uncovered, for 2–3 minutes.

3 Add the tuna, chilli sauce, if using, the olives and spaghetti. Heat well, add the seasoning and serve hot.

NUTRITION NOTES

Per portion:

Energy	306Kcals/1288kJ
Fat	2.02g
Saturated fat	0.37g
Cholesterol	48.45mg
Fibre	2.46g

BULGUR AND LENTIL PILAF

Bulgur wheat is very easy to cook and can be used in almost any way you would normally use rice, hot or cold. Some of the finer grades need hardly any cooking, so check the pack for cooking times.

INGREDIENTS

Serves 4

5ml/1 tsp olive oil
1 large onion, thinly sliced
2 garlic cloves, crushed
5ml/1 tsp ground coriander
5ml/1 tsp ground cumin
5ml/1 tsp ground turmeric
2.5ml/½ tsp ground allspice
225g/8oz/1¼ cups bulgur wheat
about 750ml/1¼ pints/3⅔ cups stock or water
115g/4oz button mushrooms, sliced
115g/4oz/⅔ cup green lentils
salt, black pepper and cayenne

1 Heat the oil in a non-stick saucepan and fry the onion, garlic and spices for 1 minute, stirring.

2 Stir in the bulgur wheat and cook, stirring, for about 2 minutes, until lightly browned. Add the stock or water, mushrooms and lentils.

3 Simmer over a very low heat for about 25–30 minutes, until the bulgur wheat and lentils are tender and all the liquid is absorbed. Add more stock or water, if necessary.

4 Season well with salt, pepper and cayenne and serve hot.

COOK'S TIP
Green lentils can be cooked without presoaking, as they cook quite quickly and keep their shape. However, if you have the time, soaking them first will shorten the cooking time slightly.

NUTRITION NOTES

Per portion:	
Energy	325Kcals/1367kJ
Fat	2.8g
Saturated fat	0.33g
Cholesterol	0
Fibre	3.61g

MINTED COUSCOUS CASTLES

Couscous is a fine semolina made from wheat grain, which is usually steamed and served plain with a rich meat or vegetable stew. Here it is flavoured with mint and moulded to make an unusual accompaniment to serve with any savoury dish.

INGREDIENTS

Serves 6
225g/8oz/1¼ cups couscous
475ml/16 fl oz/2 cups boiling stock
15ml/1 tbsp lemon juice
2 tomatoes, diced
30ml/2 tbsp chopped fresh mint
oil, for brushing
salt and black pepper
mint sprigs, to garnish

1 Place the couscous in a bowl and pour over the boiling stock. Cover the bowl and leave to stand for 30 minutes, until all the stock is absorbed and the grains are tender.

2 Stir in the lemon juice with the tomatoes and chopped mint. Adjust the seasoning with salt and pepper.

3 Brush the insides of four cups or individual moulds with oil. Spoon in the couscous mixture and pack down firmly. Chill for several hours.

4 Turn out and serve cold, or alternatively, cover and heat gently in a low oven or microwave, then turn out and serve hot, garnished with mint.

COOK'S TIP
Most packet couscous is now the ready cooked variety, which can be cooked as above, but some types need steaming first, so check the pack instructions.

NUTRITION NOTES	
Per portion:	
Energy	95Kcals/397kJ
Fat	0.53g
Saturated fat	0.07g
Cholesterol	0
Fibre	0.29g

CORN GRIDDLE PANCAKES

These crisp pancakes are delicious to serve as a snack lunch, or as a light supper with a crisp mixed salad.

INGREDIENTS

Serves 4, makes about 12
115g/4oz/1 cup self-raising flour
1 egg white
150ml/¼ pint/⅔ cup skimmed milk
200g/7oz can sweetcorn, drained
oil, for brushing
salt and black pepper
tomato chutney, to serve

1 Place the flour, egg white and skimmed milk in a food processor or blender with half the sweetcorn and process until smooth.

2 Season the batter well and add the remaining sweetcorn.

3 Heat a frying pan and brush with oil. Drop in tablespoons of batter and cook until set. Turn over the pancakes and cook the other side until golden. Serve hot with tomato chutney.

NUTRITION NOTES	
Per portion:	
Energy	162Kcals/680kJ
Fat	0.89g
Saturated fat	0.14g
Cholesterol	0.75mg
Fibre	1.49g

BAKED POLENTA WITH TOMATOES

INGREDIENTS

Serves 4
750ml/1¼ pints/3⅔ cups stock
175g/6oz/1⅛ cup polenta (coarse corn-meal)
60ml/4 tbsp chopped fresh sage
5ml/1 tsp olive oil
2 beefsteak tomatoes, sliced
15ml/1 tbsp grated Parmesan cheese
salt and black pepper

1 Bring the stock to the boil in a large saucepan, then gradually stir in the polenta.

2 Continue stirring the polenta over a moderate heat for about 5 minutes, until the mixture begins to come away from the sides of the pan. Stir in the chopped sage and season well, then spoon into a lightly oiled, shallow 23 x 33cm/9x13 in tin and spread evenly. Leave to cool.

3 Preheat the oven to 200°C/400°F/ Gas 6. Cut the cooled polenta into 24 squares using a sharp knife.

4 Arrange the polenta overlapping with tomato slices in a lightly oiled, shallow ovenproof dish. Sprinkle with Parmesan and bake for 20 minutes or until golden brown. Serve hot.

NUTRITION NOTES	
Per portion:	
Energy	200Kcals/842kJ
Fat	3.8g
Saturated fat	0.77g
Cholesterol	1.88mg
Fibre	1.71g

LEMON AND HERB RISOTTO CAKE

This unusual rice dish can be served as a main course with salad, or as a satisfying side dish. It's also good served cold, and packs well for picnics.

INGREDIENTS

Serves 4
1 small leek, thinly sliced
600ml/1 pint/2½ cups chicken stock
225g/8oz/1 cup short grain rice
finely grated rind of 1 lemon
30ml/2 tbsp chopped fresh chives
30ml/2 tbsp chopped fresh parsley
75g/3oz/¾ cup grated mozzarella cheese
salt and black pepper
parsley and lemon wedges, to garnish

1 Preheat the oven to 200°C/400°F/ Gas 6. Lightly oil a 22cm/8½ in round, loose-bottomed cake tin.

2 Cook the leek in a large pan with 45ml/3 tbsp stock, stirring over a moderate heat, to soften. Add the rice and the remaining stock.

3 Bring to the boil. Cover the pan and simmer gently, stirring occasionally, for about 20 minutes, or until all the liquid is absorbed.

4 Stir in the lemon rind, herbs, cheese and seasoning. Spoon into the tin, cover with foil and bake for 30–35 minutes or until lightly browned. Turn out and serve in slices, garnished with parsley and lemon wedges.

> **COOK'S TIP**
> The best type of rice to choose for this recipe is the Italian round grain Arborio rice, but if it is not available, use pudding rice instead.

NUTRITION NOTES

Per portion:
Energy	280Kcals/1176kJ
Fat	6.19g
Saturated fat	2.54g
Cholesterol	12.19mg
Fibre	0.9g

RICE WITH SEEDS AND SPICES

A change from plain boiled rice, and a colourful accompaniment to serve with spicy curries or grilled meats. Basmati rice gives the best texture and flavour, but you can use ordinary long grain rice instead, if you prefer.

INGREDIENTS

Serves 4

5ml/1 tsp sunflower oil
2.5ml/½ tsp ground turmeric
6 cardamom pods, lightly crushed
5ml/1 tsp coriander seeds, lightly crushed
1 garlic clove, crushed
200g/7oz/1 cup basmati rice
400ml/14 fl oz/1⅔ cups stock
115g/4oz/½ cup natural yogurt
15ml/1 tbsp toasted sunflower seeds
15ml/1 tbsp toasted sesame seeds
salt and black pepper
coriander leaves, to garnish

1 Heat the oil in a non-stick pan and fry the spices and garlic for about 1 minute, stirring all the time.

2 Add the rice and stock, bring to the boil then cover and simmer for 15 minutes or until just tender.

3 Stir in the yogurt and the toasted sunflower and sesame seeds. Adjust the seasoning and serve hot, garnished with coriander leaves.

NUTRITION NOTES

Per portion:

Energy	243Kcals/1022kJ
Fat	5.5g
Saturated fat	0.73g
Cholesterol	1.15mg
Fibre	0.57g

COOK'S TIP
Seeds are particularly rich in minerals, so they are a good addition to all kinds of dishes. Light roasting will improve their flavour.

VEGETABLES AND SALADS

We're very lucky to have a huge variety of fresh vegetables available all year round these days, so there is no excuse for not making maximum use of them in every meal, whether they form the basis of the main course, or are served as an accompaniment to meat or fish dishes. Get out of that dull daily rut of the same old familiar vegetables and try pepping them up with unusual flavours – Brussels sprouts will never be the same again when you've cooked them Chinese-style, and if you thought roast potatoes were banned, try Rosemary Roasties. Take a fresh look at salads, too, and discover that they needn't be soaked in heavy, oily dressings. Tangy natural low fat yogurt dressings or mustard and honey mixtures are light, flavourful and low in fat.

VEGETABLE RIBBONS

This may just tempt a few fussy eaters to eat up their vegetables!

INGREDIENTS

Serves 4

3 medium carrots
3 medium courgettes
120ml/4 fl oz/½ cup chicken stock
30ml/2 tbsp chopped fresh parsley
salt and black pepper

1 Using a vegetable peeler or sharp knife, cut the carrots and courgettes into thin ribbons.

2 Bring the stock to the boil in a large saucepan and add the carrots. Return the stock to the boil, then add the courgettes. Boil rapidly for 2–3 minutes, or until the vegetable ribbons are just tender.

3 Stir in the parsley, season lightly and serve hot.

NUTRITION NOTES	
Per portion:	
Energy	35Kcals/144kJ
Fat	0.53g
Saturated fat	0.09g
Cholesterol	0
Fibre	2.19g

VEGGIE BURGERS

INGREDIENTS

Serves 4

115g/4oz cup mushrooms, finely
chopped
1 small onion, chopped
1 small courgette, chopped
1 carrot, chopped
25g/1oz unsalted peanuts or cashews
115g/4oz/2 cups fresh breadcrumbs
30ml/2 tbsp chopped fresh parsley
5ml/1 tsp yeast extract
salt and black pepper
fine oatmeal or flour, for shaping

1 Cook the mushrooms in a non-stick pan without oil, stirring, for 8–10 minutes to drive off all the moisture.

2 Process the onion, courgette, carrot and nuts in a food processor until beginning to bind together.

3 Stir in the mushrooms, breadcrumbs, parsley, yeast extract and seasoning to taste. With the oatmeal or flour, shape into four burgers. Chill.

4 Cook the burgers in a non-stick frying pan with very little oil or under a hot grill for 8–10 minutes, turning once, until the burgers are cooked and golden brown. Serve hot with a crisp salad.

NUTRITION NOTES	
Per portion:	
Energy	126Kcals/530kJ
Fat	3.8g
Saturated fat	0.73g
Cholesterol	0
Fibre	2.21g

CRACKED WHEAT AND FENNEL

This salad incorporates both sweet and savoury flavours. It can be served either as a side-dish or as a starter with warm pitta bread.

NUTRITION NOTES

Per portion:

Energy	180Kcals/755kJ
Fat	6.32 g
Saturated fat	0.8g
Cholesterol	0
Fibre	2.31g

INGREDIENTS

Serves 4

115g/4oz/³/₄ cup cracked wheat
1 large fennel bulb, finely chopped
115g/4oz green beans, chopped and
    blanched
1 small orange
1 garlic clove, crushed
30ml/2 tbsp sunflower oil
15ml/1 tbsp white wine vinegar
salt and black pepper
½ red or orange pepper, seeded and
    finely chopped, to garnish

2 While still slightly warm, stir in the chopped fennel and green beans. Finely grate the orange rind into a bowl. Peel and segment the orange and stir into the salad.

1 Place the wheat in a bowl and cover with boiling water. Leave for about 10–15 minutes. Drain well and squeeze out any excess water.

3 Add the crushed garlic to the orange rind, then add the sunflower oil, white wine vinegar, and seasoning to taste, and mix thoroughly. Pour the dressing over the salad, mix well. Chill the salad for 1–2 hours.

4 Serve the salad sprinkled with the chopped red or orange pepper.

COOK'S TIP
When buying green beans, choose young, crisp ones.

SWEET POTATO AND CARROT SALAD

INGREDIENTS

Serves 4

1 sweet potato, peeled and roughly
   diced
2 carrots, cut into thick diagonal slices
3 tomatoes
8–10 iceberg lettuce leaves
75g/3oz/¾ cup canned chick-peas,
   drained

For the dressing

15ml/1 tbsp clear honey
90ml/6 tbsp low fat natural yogurt
2.5ml/½ tsp salt
5ml/1 tsp coarsely ground black pepper

For the garnish

15ml/1 tbsp walnuts
15ml/1 tbsp sultanas
1 small onion, cut into rings

NUTRITION NOTES

Per portion:	
Energy	176Kcals/741kJ
Fat	4.85g
Saturated fat	0.58g
Cholesterol	0.85mg

1 Place the potatoes in a large saucepan and cover with water. Bring to the boil and cook until soft but not mushy, cover the pan and set aside. Boil the carrots for a few minutes making sure they remain crunchy. Add to the sweet potatoes.

2 Drain the water from the sweet potatoes and carrots, and place together in a bowl.

3 Slice the tops off the tomatoes, then scoop out and discard the seeds. Roughly chop the flesh.

4 Line a glass bowl with the lettuce leaves. Mix together the sweet potatoes, carrots, chick-peas and tomatoes, and place in the bowl.

5 For the dressing, blend together all the ingredients and beat together with a fork.

6 Spoon the dressing over the salad or serve it in a separate bowl, if desired. Garnish the salad with the walnuts, sultanas and onion rings.

MASALA MASHED POTATOES

These potatoes are very versatile and will perk up any meal.

INGREDIENTS

Serves 4

3 potatoes
15ml/1 tbsp chopped fresh mint and coriander, mixed
5ml/1 tsp mango powder
5ml/1 tsp salt
5ml/1 tsp crushed black peppercorns
1 red chilli, chopped
1 green chilli, chopped
50g/2oz/4 tbsp low fat margarine

NUTRITION NOTES

Per portion:
Energy	94Kcals/394kJ
Fat	5.8g
Saturated fat	1.25g
Cholesterol	0.84mg

1 Place the potatoes in a large saucepan and cover with water. Bring to the boil and cook until soft enough to be mashed. Drain, then mash well.

2 Blend together the mint, coriander, mango powder, salt, peppercorns, chillies and margarine in a small bowl.

3 Stir the mixture into the mashed potatoes and stir together thoroughly with a fork.

4 Serve warm as an accompaniment to meat or vegetarian dishes.

> **COOK'S TIP**
> Mango powder is available in specialist Indian shops.

SPICY CABBAGE

An excellent vegetable accompaniment, this dish can also be served as a warm side salad.

INGREDIENTS

Serves 4

50g/2oz/4 tbsp low fat margarine
2.5ml/½ tsp white cumin seeds
3–8 dried red chillies, to taste
1 small onion, sliced
225g/8oz/2½ cups shredded cabbage
2 carrots, grated
2.5ml/½ tsp salt
30ml/2 tbsp lemon juice

NUTRITION NOTES

Per portion:
Energy	92Kcals/384kJ
Fat	6.06g
Saturated fat	1.28g
Cholesterol	0.84mg

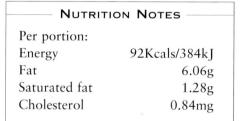

1 Melt the low fat margarine in a medium saucepan and fry the white cumin seeds and dried red chillies for about 30 seconds.

2 Add the sliced onion and fry for about 2 minutes. Add the cabbage and carrots, and stir-fry for a further 5 minutes or until the cabbage is soft.

3 Finally, stir in the salt and lemon juice, and serve either hot or warm.

RED CABBAGE IN PORT AND RED WINE

A sweet and sour, spicy red cabbage dish, with the added crunch of walnuts.

NUTRITION NOTES

Per portion:

Energy	336Kcals/1409kJ
Fat	15.41g
Saturated fat	1.58g
Cholesterol	0
Fibre	4.31g

INGREDIENTS

Serves 6

15ml/1 tbsp walnut oil
1 onion, sliced
2 whole star anise
5ml/1 tsp ground cinnamon
pinch of ground cloves
450g/1 lb/5 cups, finely shredded red
  cabbage
30ml/2 tbsp dark brown sugar
45ml/3 tbsp red wine vinegar
300ml/½ pint/1¼ cups red wine
150ml/¼ pint/⅔ cup port
2 pears, cut into 1cm/½ in cubes
115g/4oz/⅔ cup raisins
115g/4oz/½ cup walnut halves
salt and black pepper

1 Heat the oil in a large flameproof casserole. Add the onion and cook gently for about 5 minutes until softened.

2 Add the star anise, cinnamon, cloves and cabbage, and cook for a further 3 minutes.

3 Stir in the sugar, vinegar, red wine and port. Cover the pan and simmer gently for a further 10 minutes, stirring occasionally.

4 Stir in the cubed pears and raisins, and cook for a further 10 minutes or until the cabbage is tender. Season to taste. Mix in the walnut halves and serve immediately.

> **COOK'S TIP**
> If you are unable to buy prepackaged walnut halves, buy whole ones and cut them in half.

CRUSTY LEEK AND CARROT GRATIN

Tender leeks are mixed with a creamy caraway sauce and given a crunchy carrot topping.

INGREDIENTS

Serves 4–6

675g/1½ lb leeks, cut into 5cm/2 in
   pieces
150ml/¼ pint/⅔ cup vegetable stock or
   water
45ml/3 tbsp dry white wine
5ml/1 tsp caraway seeds
pinch of salt
275ml/10fl oz/1¼ cups skimmed milk,
   or as required
25g/1oz/2 tbsp sunflower margarine
25g/1oz/¼ cup plain flour

For the topping
115g/4oz/2 cups fresh wholemeal
   breadcrumbs
15g/4oz/2 cups grated carrot
30ml/2 tbsp chopped fresh parsley
75g/3oz/¾ cup coarsely grated Edam
30ml/2 tbsp flaked almonds

NUTRITION NOTES

Per portion:

Energy	314Kcals/1320kJ
Fat	15.42g
Saturated fat	6.75g
Cholesterol	30.75mg
Fibre	6.98g

1 Place the leeks in a large saucepan and add the stock or water, wine, caraway seeds and salt. Bring to a simmer, cover and cook for about 5–7 minutes until the leeks are just tender.

2 With a slotted spoon, transfer the leeks to an ovenproof dish. Boil the remaining liquid to half the original volume, then make up to 350ml/ 12fl oz/1½ cups with skimmed milk.

3 Preheat the oven to 180°C/350°F/ Gas 4. Melt the sunflower margarine in a flameproof casserole, stir in the flour and cook without allowing it to colour for about 1–2 minutes. Gradually add the stock and milk, stirring well after each addition, until you have a smooth sauce.

4 Simmer the sauce for about 5–6 minutes, stirring constantly until thickened and smooth, then pour the sauce over the leeks in the dish.

5 For the topping, mix all the ingredients together in a bowl and sprinkle over the leeks. Bake for about 20–25 minutes until golden.

Spicy Jacket Potatoes

Ingredients

Serves 2–4

2 large baking potatoes
5ml/1 tsp sunflower oil
1 small onion, finely chopped
2.5cm/1in piece fresh ginger root, grated
5ml/1 tsp ground cumin
5ml/1 tsp ground coriander
2.5ml/½ tsp ground turmeric
garlic salt
natural yogurt and fresh coriander
    sprigs, to serve

4 Cook the potato mixture for a further 2 minutes, stirring occasionally. Spoon the mixture back into the potato shells and top each with a spoonful of natural yogurt and a sprig or two of fresh coriander. Serve hot.

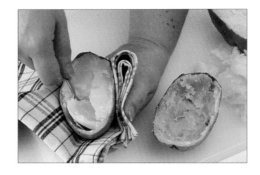

2 Cut the potatoes in half and scoop out the flesh. Heat the oil in a non-stick pan and fry the onion for a few minutes to soften. Stir in the ginger, cumin, coriander and turmeric.

Nutrition Notes

Per portion:

Energy	212Kcals/890kJ
Fat	2.54g
Saturated fat	0.31g
Cholesterol	0.4mg
Fibre	3.35g

1 Preheat the oven to 190°C/375°F/Gas 5. Prick the potatoes with a fork. Bake for 40 minutes, or until soft.

3 Stir over a low heat for about 2 minutes, then add the potato flesh, and garlic salt, to taste.

Two Beans Provençal

Ingredients

Serves 4

5ml/1 tsp olive oil
1 small onion, finely chopped
1 garlic clove, crushed
225g/8oz French beans
225g/8oz runner beans
2 tomatoes, skinned and chopped
salt and black pepper

Nutrition Notes

Per portion:

Energy	68Kcals/286kJ
Fat	1.76g
Saturated fat	0.13g
Cholesterol	0
Fibre	5.39g

1 Heat the oil in a heavy-based, or non-stick, pan and sauté the chopped onion over a medium heat until softened but not browned.

3 Cook over a fairly low heat, shaking the pan occasionally, for about 30 minutes, or until the beans are tender. Serve hot.

2 Add the garlic, the French and runner beans and the tomatoes, then season well and cover tightly.

SPRING VEGETABLE STIR-FRY

A colourful, dazzling medley of fresh, delicious and sweet young vegetables.

NUTRITION NOTES

Per portion:
Energy	106Kcals/444kJ
Fat	4.38g
Saturated fat	0.63g
Cholesterol	0
Fibre	3.86g

INGREDIENTS

Serves 4

15ml/1 tbsp groundnut oil
1 garlic clove, sliced
2.5cm/1 in piece fresh root ginger, finely chopped
115g/4oz/2 cups baby carrots
115g/4oz patty-pan squash
115g/4oz/1¼ cups baby corn
115g/4oz green beans, topped and tailed
115g/4oz/1¼ cups sugar-snap peas, topped and tailed
115g/4oz young asparagus, cut into 7.5cm/3 in pieces
8 spring onions, trimmed and cut into 5cm/2 in pieces
115g/4oz cherry tomatoes

For the dressing
juice of 2 limes
15ml/1 tbsp clear honey
15ml/1 tbsp soy sauce
5ml/1 tsp sesame oil

1 Heat the groundnut oil in a wok or large frying pan. Add the garlic and ginger and stir-fry for about 1 minute.

2 Add the carrots, patty-pan squash, baby corn and beans, and stir-fry for a further 3–4 minutes.

3 Add the sugar-snap peas, asparagus, spring onions and cherry tomatoes, and stir-fry for a further 1–2 minutes.

4 For the dressing, mix all the ingredients together and add to the pan.

5 Stir well then cover the pan. Cook for 2–3 minutes more until the vegetables are just tender but still crisp.

BEETROOT AND CELERIAC GRATIN

INGREDIENTS

Serves 6

350g/12oz raw beetroot
350g/12oz celeriac
4 thyme sprigs
6 juniper berries, crushed
120ml/4fl oz/½ cup fresh orange juice
120ml/4fl oz/½ cup vegetable stock
salt and black pepper

NUTRITION NOTES

Per portion:	
Energy	37Kcals/157kJ
Fat	0.31g
Saturated fat	0
Cholesterol	0
Fibre	3.28g

1 Preheat the oven to 190°C/375°F/ Gas 5. Peel and slice the beetroot very finely. Quarter and peel the celeriac and slice very finely.

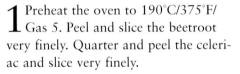

2 Fill a 25cm/10 in diameter cast iron or ovenproof frying pan with layers of beetroot and celeriac slices, sprinkling with the thyme, juniper and seasoning between each layer.

3 Mix the orange juice and stock together and pour over the gratin. Place over a medium heat and bring to the boil. Boil for about 2 minutes.

4 Cover with foil and place in the oven for about 15–20 minutes. Remove the foil and raise the oven temperature to 200°C/400°F/Gas 6. Cook for a further 10 minutes until tender. Serve garnished with a few extra crushed juniper berries and a sprig of thyme, if you like.

Bombay Spiced Potatoes

This Indian potato dish uses a wonderfully aromatic mixture of whole and ground spices. Look out for mustard and black onion seeds in specialist food shops.

INGREDIENTS

Serves 4
4 large potatoes, cut into chunks
60ml/4 tbsp sunflower oil
1 garlic clove, finely chopped
10ml/2 tsp brown mustard seeds
5ml/1 tsp black onion seeds (optional)
5ml/1 tsp turmeric
5ml/1 tsp ground cumin
5ml/1 tsp ground coriander
5ml/1 tsp fennel seeds
good squeeze of lemon juice
salt and black pepper
chopped fresh coriander and lemon
  wedges, to garnish

1 Bring a saucepan of salted water to the boil, add the potatoes and simmer for about 4 minutes, until just tender. Drain well.

2 Heat the oil in a large frying pan and add the garlic along with all the whole and ground spices. Fry gently for about 1–2 minutes, stirring until the mustard seeds start to pop.

3 Add the potatoes and stir-fry over a moderate heat for about 5 minutes, until heated through and well coated with the spicy oil.

4 Season well and sprinkle over the lemon juice. Garnish with chopped coriander and lemon wedges. Serve as an accompaniment to curries or other strong-flavoured dishes.

NUTRITION NOTES

Per portion:
Energy	373kcals/1149kJ
Fat	12.49g
Saturated fat	1.49g
Cholesterol	0
Fibre	2.65g

Spanish Chilli Potatoes

INGREDIENTS

Serves 4
1kg/2¼lb new or salad potatoes
60ml/2 tbsp olive oil
1 onion, finely chopped
2 garlic cloves, crushed
15ml/1 tbsp tomato purée
200g/7oz can chopped tomatoes
15ml/1 tbsp red wine vinegar
2–3 small dried red chillies, seeded and
  finely chopped, or 5–10ml/1–2 tsp
  hot chilli powder
5ml/1 tsp paprika
salt and black pepper
flat leaf parsley sprig, to garnish

NUTRITION NOTES

Per portion:
Energy	301Kcals/1266kJ
Fat	12.02g
Saturated fat	1.6g
Cholesterol	0
Fibre	3.54g

1 Halve the potatoes if large, then place in a large saucepan and cover with water. Bring to the boil, then simmer for about 10–12 minutes or until just tender. Drain well and leave to cool, then cut in half and reserve.

2 Heat the oil in a large pan and add the onions and garlic. Fry gently for about 5–6 minutes, until just softened. Stir in the next five ingredients, and simmer for about 5 minutes.

3 Add the potatoes and mix into the sauce mixture until well coated. Cover and simmer gently for about 8–10 minutes, or until the potatoes are tender. Season well and transfer to a warmed serving dish. Serve garnished with a sprig of flat leaf parsley.

BROCCOLI CAULIFLOWER GRATIN

Broccoli and cauliflower make an attractive combination, and this dish is much lighter than a classic cauliflower cheese.

INGREDIENTS

Serves 4
1 small cauliflower (about 250g/9oz)
1 small head broccoli (about 250g/9oz)
150g/5oz/½ cup natural low fat yogurt
75g/3oz/1 cup grated reduced fat
    Cheddar cheese
5ml/1 tsp wholegrain mustard
30ml/2 tbsp wholemeal breadcrumbs
salt and black pepper

1 Break the cauliflower and broccoli into florets and cook in lightly salted, boiling water for 8–10 minutes, until just tender. Drain well and transfer to a flameproof dish.

2 Mix together the yogurt, grated cheese and mustard, then season the mixture with pepper and spoon over the cauliflower and broccoli.

3 Sprinkle the breadcrumbs over the top and place under a moderately hot grill until golden brown. Serve hot.

COOK'S TIP
When preparing the cauliflower and broccoli, discard the tougher part of the stalk, then break the florets into even-sized pieces, so they cook evenly.

NUTRITION NOTES

Per portion:	
Energy	144Kcals/601kJ
Fat	6.5g
Saturated fat	3.25g
Cholesterol	16.5mg
Fibre	3.25g

WATERCRESS POTATO SALAD BOWL

New potatoes are equally good hot or cold, and this colourful, nutritious salad is an ideal way of making the most of them.

INGREDIENTS

Serves 4

450g/1 lb small new potatoes, unpeeled
1 bunch watercress
200g/7oz/1½ cups cherry tomatoes, halved
30ml/2 tbsp pumpkin seeds
45ml/3 tbsp low fat fromage frais
15ml/1 tbsp cider vinegar
5ml/1 tsp soft light brown sugar
salt and paprika

1 Cook the potatoes in lightly salted, boiling water until just tender, then drain and leave to cool.

2 Toss together the potatoes, water-cress, tomatoes and pumpkin seeds.

3 Place the fromage frais, vinegar, sugar, salt and paprika in a screw-topped jar and shake well to mix. Pour over the salad just before serving.

NUTRITION NOTES

Per portion:

Energy	150Kcals/630kJ
Fat	4.15g
Saturated fat	0.81g
Cholesterol	0.11mg
Fibre	2.55g

COOK'S TIP
If you are packing this salad for a picnic, take the dressing in the jar and toss in just before serving.

BEETROOT, CHICORY AND ORANGE SALAD

A refreshing salad which goes well with grilled meats or fish. Alternatively, arrange it prettily on individual plates and serve as a summer starter.

INGREDIENTS

Serves 4
2 medium cooked beetroot, diced
2 heads chicory, sliced
1 large orange
60ml/4 tbsp natural low fat yogurt
10ml/2 tsp wholegrain mustard
salt and black pepper

1 Mix together the diced cooked beetroot and sliced chicory in a large serving bowl.

2 Finely grate the rind from the orange. With a sharp knife, remove all the peel and white pith. Cut out the segments, catching the juice in a bowl. Add the segments to the salad.

3 Add the orange rind, yogurt, mustard and seasonings to the orange juice, mix thoroughly, then spoon over the salad.

> **COOK'S TIP**
> Fresh baby spinach leaves or rocket could be used in place of the chicory, if you prefer.

NUTRITION NOTES

Per portion:

Energy	41Kcals/172kJ
Fat	0.60g
Saturated fat	0.08g
Cholesterol	0.60mg
Fibre	1.42g

ROASTED PEPPER SALAD

This colourful salad is very easy and can be made up to a day in advance, as the sharp-sweet dressing mingles with the mild pepper flavours.

INGREDIENTS

Serves 4
3 large red, green and yellow peppers, halved and seeded
115g/4oz feta cheese, diced or crumbled
15ml/1 tbsp sherry vinegar or red wine vinegar
15ml/1 tbsp clear honey
salt and black pepper

1 Arrange the pepper halves in a single layer, skin side upwards, on a baking sheet. Place the peppers under a hot grill until the skin is blackened and beginning to blister.

2 Lift the peppers into a plastic bag and close the end. Leave until cool, then peel off and discard the skin.

3 Arrange the peppers on a platter and scatter the cheese over them. Mix together the vinegar, honey and seasonings, then sprinkle over the salad. Chill until ready to serve.

NUTRITION NOTES

Per portion:

Energy	110Kcals/462kJ
Fat	6.15g
Saturated fat	3.65g
Cholesterol	20.13mg
Fibre	1.84g

MIDDLE-EASTERN VEGETABLE STEW

A spiced dish of mixed vegetables which can be served as a side dish or as a vegetarian main course. Children may prefer less chilli.

INGREDIENTS

Serves 4–6
45ml/3 tbsp vegetable or chicken stock
1 green pepper, seeded and sliced
2 medium courgettes, sliced
2 medium carrots, sliced
2 celery sticks, sliced
2 medium potatoes, diced
400g/14oz can chopped tomatoes
5ml/1 tsp chilli powder
30ml/2 tbsp chopped fresh mint
15ml/1 tbsp ground cumin
400g/14oz can chick-peas, drained
salt and black pepper
mint sprigs, to garnish

1 Heat the vegetable or chicken stock in a large flameproof casserole until boiling, then add the sliced pepper, courgettes, carrot and celery. Stir over a high heat for 2–3 minutes, until the vegetables are just beginning to soften.

2 Add the potatoes, tomatoes, chilli powder, mint and cumin. Add the chick-peas and bring to the boil.

3 Reduce the heat, cover the casserole and simmer for 30 minutes, or until all the vegetables are tender. Season to taste with salt and pepper and serve hot garnished with mint leaves.

COOK'S TIP
Chick-peas are traditional in this type of Middle-Eastern dish, but if you prefer, red kidney beans or haricot beans can be used instead.

NUTRITION NOTES

Per portion:
Energy	168Kcals/703kJ
Fat	3.16g
Saturated fat	0.12g
Cholesterol	0
Fibre	6.13g

SUMMER VEGETABLE BRAISE

Tender, young vegetables are ideal for quick cooking in a minimum of liquid. Use any mixture of the family's favourite vegetables, as long as they are of similar size.

INGREDIENTS

Serves 4

175g/6oz/2½ cups baby carrots
175g/6oz/2 cups sugar-snap peas or
* mangetout*
115g/4oz/1¼ cups baby corn cobs
90ml/6 tbsp vegetable stock
10ml/2 tsp lime juice
salt and black pepper
chopped fresh parsley parsley and
* snipped fresh chives, to garnish*

1 Place the carrots, peas and baby corn cobs in a large heavy-based saucepan with the vegetable stock and lime juice. Bring to the boil.

2 Cover the pan and reduce the heat, then simmer for 6–8 minutes, shaking the pan occasionally, until the vegetables are just tender.

3 Season the vegetables to taste with salt and pepper, then stir in the chopped fresh parsley and snipped chives. Cook the vegetables for a few seconds more, stirring them once or twice until the herbs are well mixed, then serve at once with grilled lamb chops or roast chicken.

COOK'S TIP
You can make this dish in the winter too, but cut larger, tougher vegetables into chunks and cook for slightly longer.

NUTRITION NOTES

Per portion:
Energy	36Kcals/152kJ
Fat	0.45g
Saturated fat	0
Cholesterol	0
Fibre	2.35g

ROSEMARY ROASTIES

These unusual roast potatoes use far less fat than traditional roast potatoes, and because they still have their skins they not only absorb less oil but have more flavour too.

INGREDIENTS

Serves 4
1kg/2 lb small red potatoes
10ml/2 tsp walnut or sunflower oil
30ml/2 tbsp fresh rosemary leaves
salt and paprika

1 Preheat the oven to 240°C/475°F/ Gas 9. Leave the potatoes whole with the peel on, or if large, cut in half. Place the potatoes in a large pan of cold water and bring to the boil. Drain well.

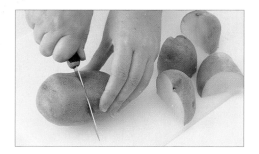

2 Drizzle the walnut or sunflower oil over the potatoes and shake the pan to coat them evenly.

3 Tip the potatoes into a shallow roasting tin. Sprinkle with rosemary, salt and paprika. Roast for 30 minutes or until crisp. Serve hot.

NUTRITION NOTES

Per portion:
Energy	205Kcals/865kJ
Fat	2.22g
Saturated fat	0.19g
Cholesterol	0
Fibre	3.25g

BAKED COURGETTES IN PASSATA

INGREDIENTS

Serves 4
5ml/1 tsp olive oil
3 large courgettes, thinly sliced
½ small red onion, finely chopped
300ml/½ pint/1¼ cups passata
30ml/2 tbsp chopped fresh thyme
garlic salt and black pepper
fresh thyme sprigs, to garnish

1 Preheat the oven to 190°C/375°F/ Gas 5. Brush an ovenproof dish with olive oil. Arrange half the courgettes and onion in the dish.

2 Spoon half the passata over the vegetables and sprinkle with some of the fresh thyme, then season to taste with garlic salt and pepper.

3 Arrange the remaining courgettes and onion in the dish on top of the passata, then season to taste with more garlic salt and pepper. Spoon over the remaining passata and spread evenly.

4 Cover the dish with foil, then bake for 40–45 minutes, or until the courgettes are tender. Garnish with sprigs of thyme and serve hot.

NUTRITION NOTES

Per portion:
Energy	49Kcals/205kJ
Fat	1.43g
Saturated fat	0.22g
Cholesterol	0
Fibre	1.73g

CHINESE SPROUTS

If you are bored with plain boiled Brussels sprouts, try pepping them up with this unusual stir-fried method, which uses the minimum of oil.

INGREDIENTS

Serves 4
450g/1 lb Brussels sprouts, shredded
5ml/1 tsp sesame or sunflower oil
2 spring onions, sliced
2.5ml/½ tsp Chinese five-spice powder
15ml/1 tbsp light soy sauce

1 Trim the Brussels sprouts, then shred them finely using a large sharp knife or shred in a food processor.

2 Heat the oil and add the sprouts and onions, then stir-fry for about 2 minutes, without browning.

3 Stir in the five-spice powder and soy sauce, then cook, stirring, for a further 2–3 minutes, until just tender.

4 Serve hot, with grilled meats or fish, or Chinese dishes.

COOK'S TIP
Brussels sprouts are rich in Vitamin C, and this is a good way to cook them to preserve the vitamins. Larger sprouts cook particularly well by this method, and cabbage can also be cooked this way.

NUTRITION NOTES

Per portion:
Energy	58Kcals/243kJ
Fat	2.38g
Saturated fat	0.26g
Cholesterol	0
Fibre	4.67g

LEMONY VEGETABLE PARCELS

Serves 4

2 medium carrots
1 small swede
1 large parsnip
1 leek, sliced
finely grated rind of ½ lemon
15ml/1 tbsp lemon juice
15ml/1 tbsp wholegrain mustard
5ml/1 tsp walnut or sunflower oil
salt and black pepper

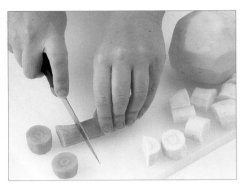

1 Preheat the oven to 190°C/375°F/ Gas 5. Peel the root vegetables and cut into 1cm/½ in cubes. Place in a large bowl, then add the sliced leek.

2 Stir the lemon rind and juice and the mustard into the vegetables and mix well, then season to taste.

3 Cut four 30cm/12 in squares of non-stick baking paper and brush lightly with the oil.

4 Divide the vegetables among them. Roll up the paper from one side, then twist the ends firmly to seal.

5 Place the parcels on a baking sheet and bake for 50–55 minutes, or until the vegetables are just tender. Serve hot with roast or grilled meats.

── **NUTRITION NOTES** ──

Per portion	
Energy	78Kcals/326kJ
Fat	2.06g
Saturated fat	0.08g
Cholesterol	0
Fibre	5.15g

NEW POTATO PARCELS

These delicious potatoes may be cooked in individual portions.

INGREDIENTS

Serves 4

16–20 very small potatoes in their skins
45ml/3 tbsp olive oil
1–2 sprigs each of thyme, tarragon and oregano, or 15ml/1 tbsp mixed dried herbs
salt and black pepper

NUTRITION NOTES

Per portion:
Energy	206Kcals/866kJ
Fat	11.49g
Saturated fat	1.54g
Cholesterol	0
Fibre	1.5g

1 Preheat the oven to 200°C/400°F/ Gas 6. Grease one large sheet or four small sheets of foil.

2 Put the potatoes in a large bowl and add in the rest of the ingredients and seasoning. Mix well so the potatoes are thoroughly coated.

3 Put the potatoes on the foil and seal up the parcel(s). Place on a baking sheet and bake for about 40–50 minutes. The potatoes will stay warm for quite some time if left wrapped up.

> COOK'S TIP
> This dish can also be cooked on a barbecue, if you like.

STIR-FRIED FLORETS WITH HAZELNUTS

INGREDIENTS

Serves 4

175g/6oz/1½ cups cauliflower florets
175g/6oz/1½ cups broccoli florets
15ml/1 tbsp sunflower oil
25g/1oz/¼ cup hazelnuts, finely chopped
¼ red chilli, finely chopped, or 5ml/ 1 tsp chilli powder (optional)
60ml/4 tbsp very low fat crème fraîche or fromage frais
salt and black pepper
a little paprika, to garnish

NUTRITION NOTES

Per portion:
Energy	146Kcals/614kJ
Fat	11.53g
Saturated fat	0.94g
Cholesterol	0.15mg
Fibre	2.84g

1 Make sure the cauliflower and broccoli florets are all of an even size. Heat the oil in a saucepan or wok and toss the florets over a high heat for 1 minute.

2 Reduce the heat and continue stir-frying for another 5 minutes, then add the hazelnuts, chilli, if using, and seasoning to taste.

3 Fry the cauliflower and broccoli florets until crisp and nearly tender, then stir in the crème fraîche or fromage frais and just heat through. Serve at once, sprinkled with the paprika.

> COOK'S TIP
> The crisper these florets are the better, so cook them just long enough to make them piping hot, and give them time to absorb all the flavours.

HOT PUDDINGS

Pudding-lovers will be glad to learn that proper puds need not be taboo for low fat diets. There are lots of ways to cook quite substantial hot puddings without the need for high-fat, rich mixtures. Classic crumbles can be made a little less sinful and far more exciting by adding less fat and more crunch in the form of oats or nuts. Skimmed or semi-skimmed milk, with a little whisked egg white, will lighten a milk pudding, and egg whites can be used in place of whole eggs for pancakes or batter puddings. For a change try an unusual couscous or breadcrumb mixture instead of a heavy sponge pudding. Even a delicious, sticky Gingerbread Upside Down Pudding can be made with just a little oil and the minimum of eggs, with no loss of pud-appeal.

FLOATING ISLANDS IN HOT PLUM SAUCE

An unusual pudding that is simpler to make than it looks. The plum sauce can be made in advance, and reheated just before you cook the meringues.

INGREDIENTS

Serves 4

450g/1 lb red plums
300ml/½ pint/1¼ cups apple juice
2 egg whites
30ml/2 tbsp concentrated apple juice
freshly grated nutmeg, to sprinkle

NUTRITION NOTES

Per portion:	
Energy	90Kcals/380kJ
Fat	0.3g
Saturated fat	0
Cholesterol	0
Fibre	1.69g

2 Bring to the boil, then cover and simmer gently until the plums have become tender.

1 Halve the plums and remove the stones. Place them in a wide saucepan, with the apple juice.

3 Meanwhile, place the egg whites in a clean, dry bowl and whisk them until they hold soft peaks.

4 Gradually whisk in the concentrated apple juice, whisking until the meringue holds fairly firm peaks.

5 Using a tablespoon, scoop the meringue mixture into the gently simmering plum sauce. You may need to cook the "islands" in two batches.

6 Cover and simmer gently for about 2–3 minutes, until the meringues are set. Serve immediately, sprinkled with a little freshly grated nutmeg.

COOK'S TIP
A bottle of concentrated apple juice is a useful storecupboard sweetener, but if you don't have any, use a little clear honey instead.

CHUNKY APPLE BAKE

This filling, economical family pudding is a good way to use up slightly stale bread – any type of bread will do, but wholemeal is richest in fibre.

INGREDIENTS

Serves 4

450g/1 lb cooking apples
75g/3oz wholemeal bread, without crusts
115g/4oz/½ cup cottage cheese
45ml/3 tbsp light brown sugar
200ml/7fl oz/⅞ cup skimmed milk
5ml/1 tsp demerara sugar

NUTRITION NOTES

Per portion:	
Energy	163Kcals/687kJ
Fat	1.75g
Saturated fat	0.84g
Cholesterol	4.74mg

1 Preheat the oven to 220°C/425°F/Gas 7. Peel the apples, cut them in quarters and remove the cores.

2 Roughly chop the apples into even-size pieces, about 1cm/½ in across.

3 Cut the bread into 1cm/½ in dice with a sharp knife.

4 Toss together the apples, bread, cottage cheese and light brown sugar.

5 Stir in the milk and then tip the mixture into a wide ovenproof dish. Sprinkle with the demerara sugar.

6 Bake for about 30–35 minutes, or until golden brown and bubbling. Serve while still hot.

COOK'S TIP
You may need to adjust the amount of milk used; the staler the bread, the more milk it will absorb.

SNOW-CAPPED APPLES

INGREDIENTS

Serves 4

4 small Bramley cooking apples
90ml/6 tbsp orange marmalade or jam
2 egg whites
50g/2oz/4 tbsp caster sugar

1 Preheat the oven to 180°C/350°F/ Gas 4. Core the apples and score through the skins around the middle with a sharp knife.

2 Place in a wide ovenproof dish and spoon 15ml/1 tbsp marmalade into the centre of each. Cover and bake for 35–40 minutes, or until tender.

3 Whisk the egg whites in a large bowl until stiff enough to hold soft peaks. Whisk in the sugar, then fold in the remaining marmalade.

4 Spoon the meringue over the apples, then return to the oven for 10–15 minutes, or until golden. Serve hot.

NUTRITION NOTES

Per portion:

Energy	165Kcals/394kJ
Fat	0.16g
Saturated fat	0
Cholesterol	0
Fibre	1.9g

STRAWBERRY APPLE TART

INGREDIENTS

Serves 4–6

150g/5oz/1¼ cups self-raising flour
50g/2oz/⅔ cup rolled oats
50g/2oz/4 tbsp sunflower margarine
2 medium Bramley cooking apples,
  about 450g/1 lb total weight
200g/7oz/2 cups strawberries, halved
50g/2oz/4 tbsp caster sugar
15ml/1 tbsp cornflour

1 Preheat the oven to 200°C/400°F/ Gas 6. Mix together the flour and oats in a large bowl and rub in the margarine evenly. Stir in just enough cold water to bind the mixture to a firm dough. Knead lightly until smooth.

2 Roll out the pastry and line a 23cm/9in loose-based flan tin. Trim the edges, prick the base and line with greaseproof paper and baking beans. Roll out the pastry trimmings and stamp out heart shapes using a cutter.

3 Bake the pastry case for 10 minutes, remove paper and beans and bake for 10–15 minutes or until golden brown. Bake the hearts until golden.

4 Peel, core and slice the apples. Place in a pan with the strawberries, sugar and cornflour. Cover and cook gently, stirring, until the fruit is just tender. Spoon into the pastry case and decorate with pastry hearts.

NUTRITION NOTES

Per portion:

Energy	382Kcals/1602kJ
Fat	11.93g
Saturated fat	2.18g
Cholesterol	0.88mg
Fibre	4.37g

GOLDEN GINGER COMPÔTE

Warm, spicy and full of sun-ripened ingredients – this is the perfect winter dessert.

INGREDIENTS

Serves 4

200g/7oz/2 cups kumquats
200g/7oz/1¼ cups dried apricots
30ml/2 tbsp sultanas
400ml/14fl oz/1⅔ cups water
1 orange
2.5cm/1 in piece fresh root ginger
4 cardamom pods
4 cloves
30ml/2 tbsp clear honey
15ml/1 tbsp flaked almonds, toasted

NUTRITION NOTES

Per portion:

Energy	196Kcals/825kJ
Fat	2.84g
Saturated fat	0.41g
Cholesterol	0
Fibre	6.82g

2 Pare the rind thinly from the orange, peel and grate the ginger, crush the cardamom pods and add to the pan, with the cloves.

1 Wash the kumquats and, if they are large, cut them in half. Place them in a saucepan with the apricots, sultanas and water. Bring to the boil.

3 Reduce the heat, cover the pan and simmer gently for about 30 minutes, or until the fruit is tender.

4 Squeeze the juice from the orange and add to the pan with honey to sweeten to taste, sprinkle with flaked almonds, and serve warm.

VARIATION

Use ready-to-eat dried apricots, but reduce the liquid to 300ml/ ½ pint/1¼ cups, and add 5 minutes before the end.

NECTARINES WITH SPICED RICOTTA

This easy dessert is good at any time of year – use canned peach halves if fresh nectarines are out of season.

INGREDIENTS

Serves 4

4 ripe nectarines or peaches
115g/4oz/½ cup ricotta cheese
15ml/1 tbsp light brown sugar
2.5ml/½ tsp ground star anise,
*   to decorate*

NUTRITION NOTES

Per portion:

Energy	92Kcals/388kJ
Fat	3.27g
Saturated fat	0
Cholesterol	14.38mg
Fibre	1.65g

1 Cut the nectarines or peaches, if using, in half and remove the stones. Do this carefully with a sharp knife and a steady hand.

2 Arrange the nectarines or peaches, cut-side upwards, in a shallow flameproof dish or on a baking sheet.

3 Place the ricotta cheese in a small mixing bowl. Stir the light brown sugar into the ricotta cheese. Using a teaspoon, spoon equal amounts of the mixture into the hollow of each nectarine or peach half.

4 Sprinkle with the star anise. Cook under a moderately hot grill for 6–8 minutes, or until the nectarines or peaches are hot. Serve warm.

COOK'S TIP
Star anise has a warm, rich flavour – if you can't get it, use ground cloves or ground allspice as an alternative.

SPICED RED FRUIT COMPOTE

Serves 4

4 ripe red plums, halved
225g/8oz/2 cups strawberries, halved
225g/8oz/1¼ cups raspberries
30ml/2 tbsp light muscovado sugar
30 ml/2 tbsp cold water
1 cinnamon stick
3 pieces star anise
6 cloves

NUTRITION NOTES

Per portion:

Energy	90Kcals/375kJ
Fat	0.32g
Saturated fat	0
Cholesterol	0
Fibre	3.38g

1 Place the plums, strawberries and raspberies in a heavy-based pan with the sugar and water.

2 Add the cinnamon stick, star anise and cloves to the pan and heat gently, without boiling, until the sugar dissolves and the fruit juices run.

3 Cover the pan and leave the fruit to infuse over a very low heat for about 5 minutes. Remove the spices from the compote before serving warm with natural yogurt or fromage frais.

RHUBARB SPIRAL COBBLER

Serves 4

675g/1½ lb rhubarb, sliced
50g/2oz/4 tbsp caster sugar
45ml/3 tbsp orange juice
200g/7oz/1⅓ cups self-raising flour
30ml/2 tbsp caster sugar
about 200g/7oz/1 cup natural yogurt
grated rind of 1 medium orange
30ml/2 tbsp demerara sugar
5ml/1 tsp ground ginger

1 Preheat the oven to 200°C/400°F/ Gas 6. Cook the rhubarb, sugar and orange juice in a covered pan until tender. Tip into an ovenproof dish.

2 To make the topping, mix the flour and caster sugar, then stir enough of the yogurt to bind to a soft dough.

3 Roll out on a floured surface to a 25cm/10in square. Mix the orange rind, demerara sugar and ginger, then sprinkle this over the dough.

4 Roll up quite tightly, then cut into about 10 slices using a sharp knife. Arrange the slices over the rhubarb.

5 Bake in the oven for 15–20 minutes, or until the spirals are well risen and golden brown. Serve warm, with yogurt or custard.

NUTRITION NOTES

Per portion:

Energy	320Kcals/1343kJ
Fat	1.2g
Saturated fat	0.34g
Cholesterol	2mg
Fibre	3.92g

Coconut and Lemon Dumplings

Ingredients

Serves 4

For the dumplings
75g/3oz/⅓ cup cottage cheese
1 egg white
25g/1oz/2 tbsp low fat margarine
15ml/1 tbsp light brown sugar
30ml/2 tbsp self-raising wholemeal
  flour
finely grated rind of ½ lemon
30ml/2 tbsp desiccated coconut,
  toasted, plus extra, to decorate

For the sauce
225g/8oz can apricot halves in natural
  juice
15ml/1 tbsp lemon juice

Nutrition Notes

Per portion:

Energy	162Kcals/681kJ
Fat	9.5g
Saturated fat	5.47g
Cholesterol	33.69mg
Fibre	2.21g

1 Half-fill a steamer with boiling water and put it on to boil, or place a heatproof dish over a saucepan of boiling water.

2 Beat together the cottage cheese, egg white and margarine.

3 Stir in the sugar, flour, lemon rind and coconut, mixing evenly to form a fairly firm dough.

4 Place eight to twelve spoonfuls of the mixture in the steamer or on the dish, leaving space between them.

5 Cover the steamer or pan tightly with a lid or a plate and steam for about 10 minutes, until the dumplings have risen and are firm to the touch.

6 Meanwhile make the sauce: put the apricots in a food processor or blender, and process until smooth. Stir in the lemon juice. Pour into a small pan and heat until boiling, then serve with the dumplings. Sprinkle with extra coconut to decorate.

BAKED APPLES IN HONEY AND LEMON

A classic mix of flavours in a healthy, traditional family pudding. Serve warm, with skimmed-milk custard.

INGREDIENTS

Serves 4

4 cooking apples
15ml/1 tbsp clear honey
grated rind and juice of 1 lemon
25g/1oz/2 tbsp low fat margarine

NUTRITION NOTES

Per portion:

Energy	71Kcals/299kJ
Fat	1.69g
Saturated fat	0.37g
Cholesterol	0.23mg
Fibre	1.93g

VARIATION

Apples are divided into dessert (or eating) and cooking apples. While cooking apples can only be used for culinary purposes because they have a sour taste, some dessert apples, especially if firm, can be used in cooking. Look for smooth-skinned apples and avoid any with brown bruises.

1 Preheat the oven to 180°C/350°F/ Gas 4. Remove the cores from the apples, leaving them whole.

2 With a canelle or sharp knife, cut lines through the apple skin at intervals and place in an ovenproof dish.

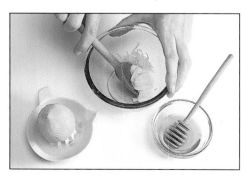

3 Mix together the honey, lemon rind and juice, and low fat margarine.

4 Spoon the mixture into the apples and cover the dish with foil or a lid. Bake for about 40–45 minutes, or until the apples are tender. Serve with custard made from skimmed milk.

COOK'S TIP

This recipe can also be cooked in the microwave to save time. Place the apples in a microwave-safe dish and cover them with a lid or pierced clear film. Microwave on FULL POWER (100%) for about 9–10 minutes.

CRISPY PEACH BAKE

A golden, crisp-crusted, family pudding that's made in minutes, from storecupboard ingredients.

INGREDIENTS

Serves 4

415g/14½oz can peach slices in juice
30ml/2 tbsp sultanas
1 cinnamon stick
strip of fresh orange rind
25g/1oz/2 tbsp low fat margarine
50g/2oz/1½ cups cornflakes
15ml/1 tbsp sesame seeds

COOK'S TIP
If you don't have a cinnamon stick, sprinkle in about 2.5ml/½ tsp ground cinnamon instead.

NUTRITION NOTES

Per portion:

Energy	184Kcals/772kJ
Fat	8.42g
Saturated fat	4.26g
Cholesterol	17.25mg

1 Drain the peaches, reserving the juice, and arrange the peach slices in a shallow ovenproof dish.

2 Preheat the oven to 200°C/400°F/Gas 6. Place the peach juice, sultanas, cinnamon stick and orange rind in a saucepan and bring to the boil. Simmer, uncovered, for about 3–4 minutes, to reduce the liquid by about half. Remove the cinnamon stick and orange rind, and spoon the syrup over the peaches.

3 Melt the low fat margarine in a small pan and stir in the cornflakes and sesame seeds.

4 Spread the cornflake mixture over the fruit. Bake for about 15–20 minutes, or until the topping is crisp and golden. Serve hot.

BAKED BLACKBERRY CHEESECAKE

This light cheesecake is best made with wild blackberries, but cultivated ones will do. You can also substitute them for other soft fruit such as raspberries or loganberries.

INGREDIENTS

Serves 5

175g/6oz/¾ cup cottage cheese
150g/5oz/⅔ cup low fat natural yogurt
15ml/1 tbsp wholemeal flour
30ml/2 tbsp golden caster sugar
1 egg
1 egg white
finely grated rind and juice of ½ lemon
200g/7oz/2 cups blackberries

NUTRITION NOTES

Per portion:

Energy	94Kcals/394kJ
Fat	1.67g
Saturated fat	1.03g
Cholesterol	5.75mg
Fibre	1.71g

1 Preheat the oven to 180°C/350°F/ Gas 4. Lightly grease and line the base of an 18cm/7 in cake tin.

2 Whizz the cottage cheese in a food processor or blender until smooth, or rub it through a sieve.

3 Add the yogurt, flour, sugar, egg and egg white, and mix. Add the lemon rind and juice, and blackberries, reserving a few for decoration.

4 Tip the mixture into the prepared tin and bake it for about 30–35 minutes, or until just set. Turn off the oven and leave for 30 minutes.

5 Run a knife around the edge of the cheesecake, and then turn it out.

6 Remove the lining paper and place the cheesecake on a warm serving plate. Decorate with the reserved blackberries and serve it warm.

COOK'S TIP
If you prefer to use canned blackberries, choose those preserved in natural juice and drain the fruit well before adding it to the cheesecake mixture. The juice may be served with the cheesecake, but this will increase the total calories.

HOT PLUM BATTER

Other fruits can be used in place of plums, depending on the season. Canned black cherries are also a convenient storecupboard substitute.

INGREDIENTS

Serves 4

450g/1 lb ripe red plums, quartered and stoned
200ml/7 fl oz/⅞ cup skimmed milk
60ml/4 tbsp skimmed milk powder
15ml/1 tbsp light muscovado sugar
5ml/1 tsp vanilla essence
75g/3oz self-raising flour
2 egg whites
icing sugar, to sprinkle

1 Preheat the oven to 220°C/425°F/ Gas 7. Lightly oil a wide, shallow ovenproof dish and add the plums.

2 Pour the milk, milk powder, sugar, vanilla, flour and egg whites into a food processor. Process until smooth.

3 Pour the batter over the plums. Bake for 25–30 minutes, or until well risen and golden. Sprinkle with icing sugar and serve immediately.

NUTRITION NOTES

Per portion:

Energy	195Kcals/816kJ
Fat	0.48g
Saturated fat	0.12g
Cholesterol	2.8mg
Fibre	2.27g

GLAZED APRICOT SPONGE

Proper puddings are usually very high in saturated fat, but this one uses the minimum of oil and no eggs.

INGREDIENTS

Serves 4

10ml/2 tsp golden syrup
411g/14½oz can apricot halves in fruit juice
150g/5oz/1¼ cup self-raising flour
75g/3oz/1½ cups fresh breadcrumbs
90g/3½oz/⅔ cup light muscovado sugar
5ml/1 tsp ground cinnamon
30ml/2 tbsp sunflower oil
175ml/6 fl oz/¾ cup skimmed milk

1 Preheat the oven to 180°C/350°F/ Gas 4. Lightly oil a 900ml/1½ pint/3¾ cup pudding basin. Spoon in the syrup.

2 Drain the apricots and reserve the juice. Arrange about 8 halves in the basin. Purée the rest of the apricots with the juice and set aside.

3 Mix the flour, breadcrumbs, sugar and cinnamon then beat in the oil and milk. Spoon into the basin and bake for 50–55 minutes, or until firm and golden. Turn out and serve with the puréed fruit as a sauce.

NUTRITION NOTES

Per portion:

Energy	364Kcals/1530kJ
Fat	6.47g
Saturated fat	0.89g
Cholesterol	0.88mg
Fibre	2.37g

CHERRY PANCAKES

INGREDIENTS

Serves 4

50g/2oz/½ cup plain flour
50g/2oz/⅓ cup wholemeal flour
pinch of salt
1 egg white
150ml/¼ pint/⅔ cup skimmed milk
150ml/¼ pint/⅔ cup water
15ml/1 tbsp sunflower oil for frying
low fat fromage frais, to serve

For the filling

425g/15oz can black cherries in juice
7.5ml/1½ tsp arrowroot

NUTRITION NOTES	
Per portion:	
Energy	173Kcals/725kJ
Fat	3.33g
Saturated fat	0.44g
Cholesterol	0.75mg
Fibre	2.36g

1 Sift the flours and salt into a bowl, adding any bran left in the sieve to the bowl at the end.

2 Make a well in the centre of the flour and add the egg white. Gradually beat in the milk and water, whisking hard until all the liquid is incorporated and the batter is smooth and frothy.

3 Heat a non-stick frying pan with a small amount of oil until the pan is very hot. Pour in just enough batter to cover the base of the pan, swirling the pan to cover the base evenly.

4 Cook until the pancake is set and golden, and then turn to cook the other side. Remove to a sheet of kitchen paper and then cook the remaining batter, to make about eight pancakes.

5 For the filling, drain the cherries, reserving the juice. Blend about 30ml/2 tbsp of the juice from the can of cherries with the arrowroot in a saucepan. Stir in the rest of the juice. Heat gently, stirring, until boiling. Stir over a moderate heat for about 2 minutes, until thickened and clear.

6 Add the cherries to the sauce and stir until thoroughly heated. Spoon the cherries into the pancakes and fold them into quarters.

> **COOK'S TIP**
> If fresh cherries are in season, cook them gently in enough apple juice just to cover them, and then thicken the juice with arrowroot as in Step 5. The basic pancakes will freeze very successfully between layers of kitchen paper or greaseproof paper.

SOUFFLÉED RICE PUDDING

INGREDIENTS

Serves 4

65g/2½oz/¼ cup short grain rice
45ml/3 tbsp clear honey
750ml/1¼ pints/3⅔ cups skimmed milk
1 vanilla pod or 2.5ml/½ tsp vanilla
  essence
2 egg whites
5ml/1 tsp freshly grated nutmeg

NUTRITION NOTES

Per portion:
Energy	163Kcals/683kJ
Fat	0.62g
Saturated fat	0.16g
Cholesterol	3.75mg
Fibre	0.08g

1 Place the rice, honey and milk in a heavy or non-stick saucepan, and bring the milk to the boil. Add the vanilla pod, if using it.

2 Reduce the heat and put the lid on the pan. Leave to simmer gently for about 1–1¼ hours, stirring occasionally to prevent sticking, until most of the liquid has been absorbed.

3 Remove the vanilla pod, or if using vanilla essence, add this to the rice mixture now. Preheat the oven to 220°C/425°F/Gas 7.

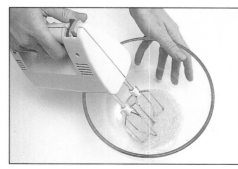

4 Place the egg whites in a clean, dry bowl and whisk them until they hold soft peaks.

5 Using either a large metal spoon or spatula, carefully fold the egg whites evenly into the rice and milk mixture and tip into a 1 litre/1¾ pint/ 4 cup ovenproof dish.

6 Sprinkle with grated nutmeg and bake for about 15–20 minutes, until the pudding is well risen and golden brown. Serve hot.

COOK'S TIP
Be very careful when simmering skimmed milk. With so little fat, it tends to boil over very easily. Use semi-skimmed if you wish.

CRUNCHY GOOSEBERRY CRUMBLE

Gooseberries are perfect for traditional family puddings like this one. When they are out of season, other fruits such as apple, plums or rhubarb could be used instead.

INGREDIENTS

Serves 4

500g/1¼ lb/5 cups gooseberries
50g/2oz/4 tbsp caster sugar
75g/3oz/1 cup rolled oats
75g/3oz/¾ cup wholemeal flour
60ml/4 tbsp sunflower oil
50g/2oz/4 tbsp demerara sugar
30ml/2 tbsp chopped walnuts
natural yogurt or custard, to serve

1 Preheat the oven to 200°C/400°F/ Gas 6. Place the gooseberries in a pan with the caster sugar. Cover the pan and cook over a low heat for 10 minutes, until the gooseberries are just tender. Tip into an ovenproof dish.

2 To make the crumble, place the oats, flour and oil in a bowl and stir with a fork until evenly mixed.

3 Stir in the demerara sugar and walnuts, then spread evenly over the gooseberries. Bake for 25–30 minutes, or until golden and bubbling. Serve hot with yogurt, or custard made with skimmed milk.

> **COOK'S TIP**
> The best cooking gooseberries are the early small, firm green ones.

NUTRITION NOTES

Per portion:	
Energy	422Kcals/1770kJ
Fat	18.5g
Saturated fat	2.32g
Cholesterol	0
Fibre	5.12g

GINGERBREAD UPSIDE DOWN PUDDING

A proper pudding goes down well on a cold winter's day. This one is quite quick to make and looks very impressive.

INGREDIENTS

Serves 4 – 6

sunflower oil, for brushing
15ml/1 tbsp soft brown sugar
4 medium peaches, halved and stoned, or canned peach halves
8 walnut halves

For the base
130g/4½oz/½ cup wholemeal flour
2.5ml/½ tsp bicarbonate of soda
7.5ml/1½ tsp ground ginger
5ml/1 tsp ground cinnamon
115g/4oz/½ cup molasses sugar
1 egg
120ml/4 fl oz/½ cup skimmed milk
50ml/2 fl oz/¼ cup sunflower oil

1 Preheat the oven to 175°C/350°F/ Gas 4. For the topping, brush the base and sides of a 23cm/9in round springform cake tin with oil. Sprinkle the sugar over the base.

2 Arrange the peaches cut-side down in the tin with a walnut half in each.

3 For the base, sift together the flour, bicarbonate of soda, ginger and cinnamon, then stir in the sugar. Beat together the egg, milk and oil, then mix into the dry ingredients until smooth.

4 Pour the mixture evenly over the peaches and bake for 35–40 minutes, until firm to the touch. Turn out onto a serving plate. Serve hot with yogurt or custard.

NUTRITION NOTES	
Per portion:	
Energy	432Kcals/1812kJ
Fat	16.54g
Saturated fat	2.27g
Cholesterol	48.72mg
Fibre	4.79g

Plum Filo Pockets

Serves 4

*115g/4oz/½ cup skimmed milk soft
  cheese*
15ml/1 tbsp light muscovado sugar
2.5ml/½ tsp ground cloves
8 large, firm plums, halved and stoned
8 sheets filo pastry
sunflower oil, for brushing
icing sugar, to sprinkle

1 Preheat the oven to 220°C/425°F/
Gas 7. Mix together the cheese,
sugar and cloves.

2 Sandwich the plum halves back
together in twos with a spoonful of
the cheese mixture.

3 Spread out the pastry and cut into
16 pieces, about 23cm/9in square.
Brush one lightly with oil and place a
second at a diagonal on top. Repeat
with the remaining squares.

4 Place a plum on each pastry square,
and pinch corners together. Place on
baking sheet. Bake for 15–18 minutes,
until golden, then dust with icing sugar.

Nutrition Notes	
Per portion:	
Energy	188Kcals/790kJ
Fat	1.87g
Saturated fat	0.27g
Cholesterol	0.29mg
Fibre	2.55g

Apple Couscous Pudding

This unusual mixture makes a
delicious family pudding with a
rich fruity flavour, but virtually
no fat.

Serves 4

600ml/1 pint/2½ cups apple juice
115g/4oz/⅔ cup couscous
40g/1½ oz/¼ cup sultanas
2.5ml/½ tsp mixed spice
*1 large Bramley cooking apple, peeled,
  cored and sliced*
30ml/2 tbsp demerara sugar
natural low fat yogurt, to serve

1 Preheat the oven to 200°C/400°F/
Gas 6. Place the apple juice, couscous, sultanas and spice in a pan and
bring to the boil, stirring. Cover and
simmer for 10–12 minutes, until all the
free liquid is absorbed.

2 Spoon half the couscous mixture
into a 1.2 litre/2 pint/5 cup ovenproof dish and top with half the apple
slices. Top with remaining couscous.

3 Arrange the remaining apple slices
overlapping over the top and sprinkle with demerara sugar. Bake for
25–30 minutes or until golden brown.
Serve hot, with yogurt.

Nutrition Notes	
Per portion:	
Energy	194Kcals/815kJ
Fat	0.58g
Saturated fat	0.09g
Cholesterol	0
Fibre	0.75g

FRUITY BREAD PUDDING

A delicious family favourite pud from grandmother's day, with a lighter, healthier touch.

INGREDIENTS

Serves 4

75g/3oz/⅗ cup mixed dried fruit
150ml/¼ pint/⅔ cup apple juice
115g/4oz stale brown or white bread, diced
5ml/1 tsp mixed spice
1 large banana, sliced
150ml/¼ pint/⅔ cup skimmed milk
15ml/1 tbsp demerara sugar
natural low fat yogurt, to serve

1 Preheat the oven to 200°C/400°F/ Gas 6. Place the dried fruit in a small pan with the apple juice and bring to the boil.

2 Remove the pan from the heat and stir in the bread, spice and banana Spoon the mixture into a shallow 1.2 litre/2 pint/5 cup ovenproof dish and pour over the milk.

3 Sprinkle with demerara sugar and bake for 25–30 minutes, until firm and golden brown. Serve hot or cold with natural yogurt.

COOK'S TIP
Different types of bread will absorb varying amounts of liquid, so you may need to adjust the amount of milk to allow for this.

NUTRITION NOTES

Per portion:

Energy	190Kcals/800kJ
Fat	0.89g
Saturated fat	0.21g
Cholesterol	0.75mg
Fibre	1.8g

SOUFFLÉED ORANGE SEMOLINA

Semolina has a poor reputation as a rather dull, sloppy pudding, but cooked like this you would hardly recognise it.

INGREDIENTS

Serves 4
50g/2oz/¼ cup semolina
600ml/1 pint/2½ cups semi-skimmed milk
30ml/2 tbsp light muscovado sugar
1 large orange
1 egg white

1 Preheat the oven to 200°C/400°F/ Gas 6. Place the semolina in a non-stick pan with the milk and sugar. Stir over a moderate heat until thickened and smooth. Remove from the heat.

2 Grate a few long shreds of orange rind from the orange and save for decoration. Finely grate the remaining rind. Cut all the peel and white pith from the orange and remove the segments. Stir into the semolina with the orange rind.

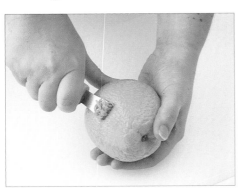

3 Whisk the egg white until stiff but not dry, then fold lightly and evenly into the mixture. Spoon into a 1 litre/ 1¾ pint/4 cup ovenproof dish and bake for 15–20 minutes, until risen and golden brown. Serve immediately.

COOK'S TIP
When using the rind of citrus fruit, scrub the fruit thoroughly before use, or buy unwaxed fruit.

NUTRITION NOTES

Per portion:
Energy	158Kcals/665kJ
Fat	2.67g
Saturated fat	1.54g
Cholesterol	10.5mg
Fibre	0.86g

Banana, Maple and Lime Pancakes

Pancakes are a treat any day of the week, and they can be made in advance and stored in the freezer for convenience.

INGREDIENTS

Serves 4
115g/4oz/1 cup plain flour
1 egg white
250ml/8 fl oz/1 cup skimmed milk
50ml/2 fl oz/¼ cup cold water
sunflower oil, for frying

For the filling
4 bananas, sliced
45ml/3 tbsp maple syrup or golden syrup
30ml/2 tbsp lime juice
strips of lime rind, to decorate

1 Beat together the flour, egg white, milk and water until smooth and bubbly. Chill until needed.

2 Heat a small amount of oil in a non-stick frying pan and pour in enough batter just to coat the base. Swirl it around the pan to coat evenly.

3 Cook until golden, then toss or turn and cook the other side. Place on a plate, cover with foil and keep hot while making the remaining pancakes.

4 To make the filling, place the bananas, syrup and lime juice in a pan and simmer gently for 1 minute. Spoon into the pancakes and fold into quarters. Sprinkle with shreds of lime rind to decorate. Serve hot, with yogurt or low fat fromage frais.

> **COOK'S TIP**
> Pancakes freeze well. To store for later use, interleave them with non-stick baking paper, overwrap and freeze for up to 3 months.

NUTRITION NOTES

Per portion:

Energy	282Kcals/1185kJ
Fat	2.79g
Saturated fat	0.47g
Cholesterol	1.25mg
Fibre	2.12g

SPICED PEARS IN CIDER

Any variety of pear can be used for cooking, but it is best to choose firm pears for this recipe, or they will break up easily – Conference are a good choice.

INGREDIENTS

Serves 4

4 *medium firm pears*
250ml/8 fl oz/1 cup dry cider
thinly pared strip of lemon rind
1 *cinnamon stick*
30ml/2 tbsp light muscovado sugar
5ml/1 tsp arrowroot
ground cinnamon, to sprinkle

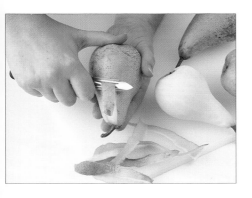

1 Peel the pears thinly, leaving them whole with the stalks on. Place in a pan with the cider, lemon rind and cinnamon. Cover and simmer gently, turning the pears occasionally for 15–20 minutes, or until tender.

2 Lift out the pears. Boil the syrup, uncovered to reduce by about half. Remove the lemon rind and cinnamon stick, then stir in the sugar.

3 Mix the arrowroot with 15ml/ 1 tbsp cold water in a small bowl until smooth, then stir into the syrup. Bring to the boil and stir over the heat until thickened and clear.

4 Pour the sauce over the pears and sprinkle with ground cinnamon. Leave to cool slightly, then serve warm with low fat fromage frais.

COOK'S TIP
Whole pears look very impressive, but if you prefer, they can be halved and cored before cooking. This will shorten the cooking time slightly.

NUTRITION NOTES

Per portion:

Energy	102Kcals/428kJ
Fat	0.18g
Saturated fat	0.01g
Cholesterol	0
Fibre	1.65g

COLD DESSERTS

From fresh, colourful fruit salads to refreshing, tangy sorbets, healthy cold desserts should be the easiest part of selecting dishes for your low fat menus. The year-round huge variety of fresh fruit gives a head start – even the simplest platter of fresh fruits can make an exotic dessert. Time was when ice creams, mousses and cheesecakes were without exception rich, elaborate and high fat, certainly to be avoided in excess. But the rapidly expanding range of low fat dairy products such as fromage frais, yogurts, and crème fraîche, means that lighter, far less rich versions are now possible. So, if plain fresh fruit is just not enough, you can tuck into a luscious scoop of Banana Honey Yogurt Ice or a slice of Creamy Mango Cheesecake with not a trace of guilt.

Fluffy Banana and Pineapple Mousse

This light, low fat mousse looks very impressive but is really very easy to make, especially with a food processor. You could try substituting the canned pineapple chunks for other canned fruits such as peaches or apricots.

Ingredients

Serves 6

2 ripe bananas
225g/8oz/1 cup cottage cheese
425g/15oz can pineapple chunks or pieces in juice
15ml/1 tbsp/1 sachet powdered gelatine
2 egg whites

Nutrition Notes

Per portion:

Energy	110Kcals/464kJ
Fat	1.6g
Saturated fat	0.98g
Cholesterol	4.88mg
Fibre	0.51g

1 Tie a double band of non-stick baking paper around a 600ml/1 pint/2½ cup soufflé dish, to come 5cm/2 in above the rim.

2 Peel and chop one banana and place it in a food processor or blender with the cottage cheese. Process until smooth.

3 Drain the pineapple, reserving the juice, and reserve a few pieces or chunks for decoration. Add the rest to the banana mixture and process for a few seconds until finely chopped. Transfer the mixture to a large bowl.

4 Dissolve the gelatine in 60ml/4 tbsp of the reserved pineapple juice. Stir the gelatine quickly into the fruit mixture with a spoon.

5 In a separate bowl, quickly whisk the egg whites until they hold soft peaks, then fold them lightly and evenly into the fruit mixture. Tip the mousse into the prepared dish, smooth the surface and chill until set.

6 When the mousse is set, carefully remove the paper collar. Decorate the mousse with the reserved banana and pineapple.

> **Cook's Tip**
> For a simpler way of serving, use a 1 litre/1¾ pint/4 cup serving dish, but do not tie a collar around the edge.

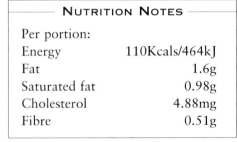

ROSE-SCENTED FRUIT COMPÔTE

Rose-scented tea gives this dessert a lovely subtle flavour.

INGREDIENTS

Serves 4

5ml/1 tsp rose pouchong tea
5ml/1 tsp rose water (optional)
50g/2oz/¼ cup sugar
5ml/1 tsp lemon juice
5 dessert apples
175g/6oz/1½ cups fresh raspberries

NUTRITION NOTES

Per portion:

Energy	141Kcals/591kJ
Fat	0.34g
Saturated fat	0
Cholesterol	0
Fibre	3.94g

1 Warm a large tea pot. Add the rose pouchong tea and 900ml/1½ pints/3¾ cups of boiling water together with the rose water, if using. Allow to stand and infuse for about 4 minutes.

2 Measure the sugar and lemon juice into a stainless steel saucepan. Strain in the tea and stir to dissolve the sugar.

3 Peel and quarter the apples, then remove the cores.

4 Add the apples to the syrup and poach for about 5 minutes.

5 Transfer the apples and syrup to a large metal baking tray and leave to cool to room temperature.

6 Pour the cooled apples and syrup into a bowl, add the raspberries and mix to combine. Spoon into individual glass dishes or bowls and serve.

COOK'S TIP
If fresh raspberries are out of season, use the same weight of frozen fruit or a 400g/14oz can of well-drained fruit.

CREAMY MANGO CHEESECAKE

Cheesecakes are always a favourite but sadly they are often high in fat. This one is the exception.

INGREDIENTS

Serves 4
115g/4oz/1¼ cups rolled oats
40g/1½oz/3 tbsp sunflower margarine
30ml/2 tbsp clear honey
1 large ripe mango
300g/10oz/1¼ cups low fat soft cheese
150g/5oz/⅔ cup low fat natural yogurt
finely grated rind of 1 small lime
45ml/3 tbsp apple juice
20ml/4 tsp powdered gelatine
fresh mango and lime slices, to decorate

1 Preheat the oven to 200°C/400°F/ Gas 6. Mix together the oats, margarine and honey. Press the mixture into the base of a 20cm/8in loose-bottomed cake tin. Bake for 12–15 minutes, until lightly browned. Cool.

2 Peel, stone and roughly chop the mango. Place the chopped mango, cheese, yogurt and lime rind in a food processor and process until smooth.

3 Heat the apple juice until boiling, sprinkle the gelatine over it, stir to dissolve, then stir into cheese mixture.

4 Pour the cheese mixture into the tin and chill until set, then turn out on to a serving plate. Decorate the top with mango and lime slices.

NUTRITION NOTES	
Per portion:	
Energy	422Kcals/1774kJ
Fat	11.37g
Saturated fat	2.2g
Cholesterol	2.95mg
Fibre	7.15g

FRUDITÉS WITH HONEY DIP

INGREDIENTS

Serves 4
225g/8oz/1 cup Greek-style yogurt
45ml/3 tbsp clear honey
selection of fresh fruit for dipping such as apples, pears, tangerines, grapes, figs, cherries, strawberries and kiwi fruit

NUTRITION NOTES	
Per portion:	
Energy	161Kcals/678kJ
Fat	5.43g
Saturated fat	3.21g
Cholesterol	7.31mg
Fibre	2.48g

1 Place the yogurt in a dish, beat until smooth, then stir in the honey, leaving a little marbled effect.

2 Cut the fruits into wedges or bite-sized pieces or leave whole.

3 Arrange the fruits on a platter with the bowl of dip in the centre. Serve chilled.

YOGURT RING WITH TROPICAL FRUIT

INGREDIENTS

Serves 6

175ml/6fl oz/³/₄ cup tropical fruit juice
15ml/1 tbsp/1 sachet powdered
  gelatine
3 egg whites
150g/5oz/²/₃ cup low fat natural yogurt
finely grated rind of 1 lime

For the filling
1 mango
2 kiwi fruit
10–12 cape gooseberries
juice of 1 lime

NUTRITION NOTES

Per portion:	
Energy	98Kcals/410kJ
Fat	0.57g
Saturated fat	0.13g
Cholesterol	1mg
Fibre	2.72g

1 Place the fruit juice in a saucepan and sprinkle the gelatine over. Heat gently until the gelatine has dissolved.

2 Whisk the egg whites in a clean, dry bowl until they hold soft peaks. Continue whisking hard, whilst gradually adding the yogurt and lime rind.

3 Continue whisking hard and pour in the hot gelatine mixture.

4 Mix the gelatine mixture until everything is mixed in. Quickly pour the mixture into a 1.5 litre/2½ pint/6¼ cup ring mould. Chill the mould in the fridge until set. The mixture will separate into two layers.

5 For the filling, halve, stone, peel and dice the mango. Peel and slice the kiwi fruit. Remove the outer leaves from the cape gooseberries and cut in half. Toss all the fruits together and stir in the lime juice.

6 Run a knife around the edge of the ring to loosen the mixture. Dip the mould quickly into cold water and then turn it out on to a serving plate. Spoon all the prepared fruit into the centre of the ring and serve immediately.

SUMMER FRUIT SALAD ICE CREAM

This beautiful ice cream contains delicious mixed summer fruits.

INGREDIENTS

Serves 6

900g/2 lb/8 cups mixed soft summer fruit, such as raspberries, strawberries, blackcurrants and redcurrants
2 eggs, separated
225g/8oz/1 cup low fat Greek-style yogurt
175ml/6fl oz/³⁄4 cup red grape juice
15ml/1 tbsp/1 sachet powdered gelatine

NUTRITION NOTES

Per portion:

Energy	133Kcals/558kJ
Fat	5.69g
Saturated fat	2.72g
Cholesterol	78.02mg
Fibre	3.6g

1 Reserve half the fruit and purée the rest in a food processor or blender, or rub it through a sieve to make a smooth purée.

2 Whisk the egg yolks and yogurt into the fruit purée.

3 Heat the grape juice until almost boiling. Remove from the heat, sprinkle the gelatine over the juice and stir to dissolve the gelatine completely.

4 Whisk the dissolved gelatine into the fruit purée. Pour into a freezer container. Freeze until slushy.

5 Whisk the egg whites until they are stiff. Quickly fold them into the half-frozen mixture.

6 Return to the freezer and freeze until almost firm. Scoop into individual dishes or glasses and decorate with the reserved soft fruits.

> **COOK'S TIP**
> Red grape juice has a good flavour and improves the colour of the ice, but if it is not available, use cranberry, apple or orange juice instead.

GRAPE CHEESE WHIP

INGREDIENTS

Serves 4

150g/5oz/1 cup black or green seed-
less grapes, plus 4 sprigs
2 egg whites
15ml/1 tbsp caster sugar
finely grated rind and juice of ½ lemon
225g/8oz/1 cup skimmed milk soft
cheese
45ml/3 tbsp clear honey
30ml/2 tbsp brandy (optional)

NUTRITION NOTES

Per portion:
Energy	135Kcals/563kJ
Fat	0
Saturated fat	0
Cholesterol	0.56mg
Fibre	0

1 Brush the sprigs of grapes lightly with egg white and sprinkle with sugar to coat. Leave to dry.

2 Mix together the lemon rind and juice, cheese, honey and brandy. Chop the remaining grapes and stir in.

3 Whisk the egg whites until stiff enough to hold soft peaks. Fold the whites into the grape mixture, then spoon into serving glasses.

4 Top with sugar-frosted grapes and serve chilled.

STRAWBERRIES IN SPICED GRAPE JELLY

INGREDIENTS

Serves 4

450ml/¾ pint/1⅞cups red grape juice
1 cinnamon stick
1 small orange
15ml/1 tbsp/1 envelope gelatine
225g/8oz strawberries, chopped
strawberries and orange rind, to
decorate

1 Place the grape juice in a pan with the cinnamon. Thinly pare the rind from the orange and add to the pan. Infuse over a very low heat for 10 minutes, then remove the flavourings.

2 Squeeze the juice from the orange and sprinkle over the gelatine. Stir into the grape juice to dissolve. Allow to cool until just beginning to set.

3 Stir in the strawberries and quickly tip into a 1 litre/1¾pint/4 cup mould or serving dish. Chill until set.

4 To turn out, dip the mould quickly into hot water and invert on to a serving plate. Decorate with fresh strawberries and shreds of orange rind.

NUTRITION NOTES

Per portion:
Energy	85Kcals/355kJ
Fat	0.2g
Saturated fat	0
Cholesterol	0
Fibre	1.04g

Pears in Maple and Yogurt Sauce

Serves 6
6 *firm pears*
15ml/1 tbsp lemon juice
250ml/8fl oz/1 cup sweet white wine or cider
thinly pared rind of 1 lemon
1 cinnamon stick
30ml/2 tbsp maple syrup
2.5ml/½ tsp arrowroot
150g/5oz/⅔ cup low fat Greek-style yogurt

Nutrition Notes

Per portion:
Energy	132Kcals/556kJ
Fat	2.4g
Saturated fat	1.43g
Cholesterol	3.25mg
Fibre	2.64g

1 Thinly peel the pears, leaving them whole and with stalks intact. Brush them with lemon juice, to prevent them from browning. Use a potato peeler or small knife to scoop out the core from the base of each pear.

2 Place the pears in a wide, heavy saucepan and pour over the wine or cider, with enough cold water almost to cover the pears.

3 Add the lemon rind and cinnamon stick, and then bring to the boil. Reduce the heat, and simmer the pears gently for about 30–40 minutes, or until tender. Turn the pears occasionally. Lift the pears out carefully, draining them well.

4 Bring the liquid to the boil and boil uncovered to reduce to about 120ml/4fl oz/½ cup.

5 Strain the liquid and add the maple syrup. Blend a little of the liquid with the arrowroot. Return to the pan and cook, stirring, until thick and clear. Leave to cool.

6 Slice each pear about three-quarters of the way through, leaving the slices attached at the stem end. Fan each pear out on a serving plate.

7 Stir 30ml/2 tbsp of the cooled syrup into the yogurt and spoon it around the pears. Drizzle with the remaining syrup and serve immediately.

Cook's Tip
Poach the pears in advance, and have the cooled syrup ready to spoon on to the plates just before serving. The cooking time of this dish will vary, depending upon the type and ripeness of the pears. The pears should be ripe, but still firm – over-ripe ones will not keep their shape well.

ICED APPLE AND BLACKBERRY TERRINE

Apples and blackberries are a classic autumn combination; they really complement each other. This pretty, three-layered terrine is frozen, so you can enjoy it at any time of year.

INGREDIENTS

Serves 6
450g/1 lb cooking or eating apples
300ml/½ pint/1¼ cups sweet cider
15ml/1 tbsp clear honey
5ml/1 tsp vanilla essence
200g/7oz/2 cups fresh or frozen and
  thawed blackberries
15ml/1 tbsp/1 sachet powdered gelatine
2 egg whites
fresh apple slices and blackberries,
  to decorate

NUTRITION NOTES

Per portion:
Energy	78Kcals/328kJ
Fat	0.18g
Saturated fat	0
Cholesterol	0
Fibre	2.37g

1 Peel, core and chop the apples, and place them in a saucepan with half the cider. Bring to the boil, then cover the pan and simmer gently until tender.

2 Tip the apples into a food processor or blender and process to a smooth purée. Stir in the honey and vanilla. Add half the blackberries to half the apple purée, and process again until smooth. Sieve to remove the pips.

3 Heat the remaining cider until almost boiling, then sprinkle the gelatine over and stir until the gelatine has completely dissolved. Add half the gelatine to the apple purée and half to the blackberry purée.

4 Leave the purées to cool until almost set. Whisk the egg whites until they are stiff. Quickly fold them into the apple purée. Remove half the purée to another bowl. Stir the remaining whole blackberries into half the apple purée, and then tip this into a 1.75 litre/3 pint/7½ cup loaf tin, packing it down firmly.

5 Top with the blackberry purée and spread it evenly. Finally, add a layer of the apple purée and smooth it evenly. (If necessary, freeze each layer until firm before adding the next.)

6 Freeze until firm. To serve, allow to stand at room temperature for 20 minutes to soften, then place slices, decorated with fresh apple slices and blackberries, on individual plates.

> **COOK'S TIP**
> To set without layering, purée the apples and blackberries together, stir in the dissolved gelatine and whisked egg whites, turn into the tin and leave to set.

FRESH CITRUS JELLY

Fresh fruit jellies really are worth the effort – they make a stunning fat-free dessert and are also rich in vitamins.

INGREDIENTS

Serves 4
3 oranges
1 lemon
1 lime
300ml/½ pint/1¼ cups water
75g/3oz/⅓ cup golden caster sugar
15ml/1 tbsp/1 sachet powdered gelatine
extra slices of fruit, to decorate

NUTRITION NOTES

Per portion:
Energy	136Kcals/573kJ
Fat	0.21g
Saturated fat	0
Cholesterol	0
Fibre	2.13g

1 With a sharp knife, cut all the peel and white pith from one orange and carefully remove the segments. Arrange all of the segments in the base of a 900ml/1½ pint/3¾ cup mould or dish.

2 Remove some shreds of citrus rind with a zester and reserve them for decoration. Grate the remaining rind from the lemon and lime and one orange. Place all the grated rind in a saucepan with the water and sugar.

3 Heat gently until the sugar has dissolved. Remove from the heat. Squeeze the juice from all the rest of the fruit and stir it into the pan.

4 Strain the liquid into a measuring jug to remove the rind (you should have about 600ml/1 pint/2½ cups: if necessary, make up the amount with water). Sprinkle the gelatine over the liquid and stir until dissolved.

5 Pour a little of the jelly over the orange segments and chill until it has set. Leave the remaining jelly at room temperature to cool, but do not allow it to set.

6 Pour the remaining cooled jelly into the dish and chill until set. To serve, turn out the jelly and decorate it with the reserved citrus rind shreds and slices of citrus fruit.

> **COOK'S TIP**
> To speed up the setting of the fruit segments in jelly, stand the dish in a bowl of ice.

SPICED PINEAPPLE WEDGES WITH LIME

Fresh pineapple is easy to prepare and always looks very festive, so this dish is perfect for easy entertaining.

INGREDIENTS

Serves 4

1 ripe pineapple
1 lime
15ml/1 tbsp dark muscovado sugar
5ml/1 tsp ground allspice

NUTRITION NOTES

Per portion:

Energy	71Kcals/296kJ
Fat	0.39 g
Saturated fat	0.03g
Cholesterol	0
Fibre	1.5g

VARIATION

For a quick hot dish, place the pineapple slices on a baking sheet, sprinkle them with the lime juice, sugar and allspice, and place them under a hot grill for about 3–4 minutes, or until golden and bubbling. Sprinkle with shreds of lime zest and serve.

2 Loosen the flesh with a sharp knife. Cut the flesh into slices, leaving it on the skin.

4 Sprinkle the pineapple with the lime juice and zest, sugar and allspice. Serve immediately, or for better results chill for up to an hour.

COOK'S TIP

When buying a fresh pineapple, choose a fruit with stiff leaves. Pineapples can be used to make a variety of desserts, and their shells make attractive containers for fruit salads, pineapple sorbet and ice creams.

1 Cut the pineapple lengthways into quarters and remove the core. Make sure you use a sharp knife and hold the pineapple firmly.

3 Remove some shreds of rind from the lime and squeeze.

EMERALD FRUIT SALAD

INGREDIENTS

Serves 4

30ml/2 tbsp lime juice
30ml/2 tbsp clear honey
2 green eating apples, cored and sliced
1 small ripe Ogen melon, diced
2 kiwi fruit, sliced
1 star fruit, sliced
mint sprigs, to decorate

1 Mix together the lime juice and honey in a large bowl, then toss the apple slices in this.

2 Stir in the melon, kiwi fruit and star fruit. Place in a glass serving dish and chill before serving.

3 Decorate with mint sprigs and serve with yogurt or fromage frais.

COOK'S TIP
Starfruit is best when fully ripe – look for plump, yellow fruit.

NUTRITION NOTES

Per portion:

Energy	93Kcals/390kJ
Fat	0.48g
Saturated fat	0
Cholesterol	0
Fibre	2.86g

PEACH AND GINGER PASHKA

This simpler adaptation of a Russian Easter favourite is made with much lighter ingredients than the traditional version.

INGREDIENTS

Serves 4–6

350g/12oz/1½ cups low fat cottage
    cheese
2 ripe peaches or nectarines
90g/3½oz/⅓ cup low fat natural yogurt
2 pieces stem ginger in syrup, drained
    and chopped
30ml/2 tbsp stem ginger syrup
2.5ml/½ tsp vanilla essence
peach slices and toasted flaked
    almonds, to decorate

NUTRITION NOTES

Per portion:

Energy	142Kcals/600kJ
Fat	1.63g
Saturated fat	0.22g
Cholesterol	1.77mg
Fibre	1.06g

1 Drain the cottage cheese and rub through a sieve into a bowl. Stone and roughly chop the peaches.

2 Mix together the chopped peaches, cottage cheese, yogurt, ginger, syrup and vanilla essence.

3 Line a new, clean flowerpot or a sieve with a piece of clean, fine cloth such as muslin.

4 Tip in the cheese mixture, then wrap over the cloth and place a weight on top. Leave over a bowl in a cool place to drain overnight. To serve, unwrap the cloth and invert the pashka on to a plate. Decorate with peach slices and almonds.

PLUM AND PORT SORBET

Rather a grown-up sorbet, this one, but you could use fresh, still red grape juice in place of the port if you prefer.

INGREDIENTS

Serves 4–6
1kg/2 lb ripe red plums, halved and
stoned
75g/3oz/6 tbsp caster sugar
45ml/3 tbsp water
45ml/3 tbsp ruby port or red wine
crisp, sweet biscuits, to serve

1 Place the plums in a pan with the sugar and water. Stir over a gentle heat until the sugar is melted, then cover and simmer gently for about 5 minutes, until the fruit is soft.

2 Turn into a food processor and purée until smooth, then stir in the port. Cool completely, then tip into a freezer container and freeze until firm around the edges.

3 Spoon into the food processor and process until smooth. Return to the freezer and freeze until solid.

4 Allow to soften slightly at room temperature for 15–20 minutes before serving in scoops, with sweet biscuits.

NUTRITION NOTES	
Per portion:	
Energy	166Kcals/699kJ
Fat	0.25g
Saturated fat	0
Cholesterol	0
Fibre	3.75g

TOFU BERRY BRULÉE

This is a lighter variation of a classic dessert, usually forbidden on a low fat diet, using tofu, which is low in fat and free from cholesterol. Use any soft fruits in season.

INGREDIENTS

Serves 4

300g/11oz packet silken tofu
45ml/3 tbsp icing sugar
225g/8oz/1½ cups red berry fruits,
 such as raspberries, strawberries and
 redcurrants
about 75ml/5 tbsp demerara sugar

1 Place the tofu and icing sugar in a food processor or blender and process until smooth.

2 Stir in the fruits and spoon into a 900ml/1½ pint/3¾ cup flameproof dish. Sprinkle the top with enough demerara sugar to cover evenly.

3 Place under a very hot grill until the sugar melts and caramelises. Chill before serving.

COOK'S TIP
Choose silken tofu rather than firm tofu as it gives a smoother texture in this type of dish. Firm tofu is better for cooking in chunks.

NUTRITION NOTES	
Per portion:	
Energy	180Kcals/760kJ
Fat	3.01g
Saturated fat	0.41g
Cholesterol	0
Fibre	1.31g

APRICOT MOUSSE

This light, fluffy dessert can be made with any dried fruits instead of apricots – try dried peaches, prunes or apples.

INGREDIENTS

Serves 4

300g/10oz/1½ cups ready-to-eat dried
   apricots
300ml/½ pint/1¼ cups fresh orange
   juice
200g/7oz/⅞ cup low fat fromage frais
2 egg whites
mint sprigs, to decorate

1 Place the apricots in a saucepan with the orange juice and heat gently until boiling. Cover and simmer gently for 3 minutes.

2 Cool slightly. Place in a food processor or blender and process until smooth. Stir in the fromage frais.

3 Whisk the egg whites until stiff enough to hold soft peaks, then fold into the apricot mixture.

4 Spoon into four stemmed glasses or one large serving dish. Chill before serving.

COOK'S TIP
To make a speedier fool-type dish, omit the egg whites and simply swirl together the apricot mixture and fromage frais.

NUTRITION NOTES

Per portion:

Energy	180Kcals/757kJ
Fat	0.63g
Saturated fat	0.06g
Cholesterol	0.5mg
Fibre	4.8g

APPLE FOAM WITH BLACKBERRIES

Any seasonal soft fruit can be used for this if blackberries are not available.

INGREDIENTS

Serves 4

225g/8oz blackberries
150ml/¼ pint/⅔ cup apple juice
5ml/1 tsp powdered gelatine
15ml/1 tbsp clear honey
2 egg whites

1 Place the blackberries in a pan with 60ml/4 tbsp of the apple juice and heat gently until the fruit is soft. Remove from the heat, cool and chill.

2 Sprinkle the gelatine over the remaining apple juice in a small pan and stir over a low heat until dissolved. Stir in the honey.

3 Whisk the egg whites until they hold stiff peaks. Continue whisking hard and pour in the hot gelatine mixture gradually, until well mixed.

4 Quickly spoon the foam into rough mounds on individual plates. Chill. Serve with the blackberries and juice spooned around.

COOK'S TIP
Make sure that you dissolve the gelatine over a very low heat. It must not boil, or it will lose its setting ability.

NUTRITION NOTES

Per portion:

Energy	49Kcals/206kJ
Fat	0.15g
Saturated fat	0
Cholesterol	0
Fibre	1.74g

Banana Honey Yogurt Ice

Ingredients

Serves 4–6

4 ripe bananas, chopped roughly
15ml/1 tbsp lemon juice
30ml/2 tbsp clear honey
250g/9oz/1 cup Greek-style yogurt
2.5ml/½ tsp ground cinnamon
crisp biscuits, flaked hazelnuts and
   banana slices, to serve

Nutrition Notes

Per portion:

Energy	138Kcals/580kJ
Fat	7.37g
Saturated fat	3.72g
Cholesterol	8.13mg
Fibre	0.47g

1 Place the bananas in a food processor or blender with the lemon juice, honey, yogurt and cinnamon. Process until smooth and creamy.

2 Pour the mixture into a freezer container and freeze until almost solid. Spoon back into the food processor and process again until smooth.

3 Return to the freezer until firm. Allow to soften at room temperature for 15 minutes, then serve in scoops, with crisp biscuits, flaked hazelnuts and banana slices.

Autumn Pudding

Ingredients

Serves 6

10 slices white or brown bread, at least
   1 day old
1 Bramley cooking apple, peeled, cored
   and sliced
225g/8oz ripe red plums, halved and
   stoned
225g/8oz blackberries
60ml/4 tbsp water
75g/3oz/6 tbsp caster sugar

1 Remove the crusts from the bread and use a biscuit cutter to stamp out a 7.5cm/3in round from one slice. Cut the remaining slices in half.

2 Place the bread round in the base of a 1.2 litre/2 pint/5 cup pudding basin, then overlap the fingers around the sides, saving some for the top.

3 Place the apple, plums, blackberries, water and sugar in a pan, heat gently until the sugar dissolves, then simmer gently for 10 minutes, or until soft. Remove from the heat.

4 Reserve the juice and spoon the fruit into the bread-lined basin. Top with the reserved bread, then spoon over the reserved fruit juices.

5 Cover the mould with a saucer and place weights on top. Chill the pudding overnight. Turn out on to a serving plate and serve with low fat yogurt or fromage frais.

Nutrition Notes

Per portion:

Energy	197Kcals/830kJ
Fat	1.1g
Saturated fat	0.2g
Cholesterol	0
Fibre	2.84g

FRUITED RICE RING

This unusual rice pudding looks beautiful turned out of a ring mould but if you prefer, stir the fruit into the rice and serve in individual dishes.

INGREDIENTS

Serves 4

65g/2½oz/5 tbsp short grain rice
900ml/1½ pint/3¾ cups semi-skimmed milk
1 cinnamon stick
175g/6oz/1½ cups dried fruit salad
175ml/6 fl oz/¾ cup orange juice
45ml/3 tbsp caster sugar
finely grated rind of 1 small orange

1 Place the rice, milk and cinnamon stick in a large pan and bring to the boil. Cover and simmer, stirring occasionally, for about 1½ hours, until no free liquid remains.

2 Meanwhile, place the fruit and orange juice in a pan and bring to the boil. Cover and simmer very gently for about 1 hour, until tender and no free liquid remains.

3 Remove the cinnamon stick from the rice and stir in the sugar and orange rind.

4 Tip the fruit into the base of a lightly oiled 1.5 litre/2½ pint/6 cup ring mould. Spoon the rice over, smoothing down firmly. Chill.

5 Run a knife around the edge of the mould and turn out the rice carefully on to a serving plate.

NUTRITION NOTES

Per portion:

Energy	343Kcals/1440kJ
Fat	4.4g
Saturated fat	2.26g
Cholesterol	15.75mg
Fibre	1.07g

RASPBERRY PASSION FRUIT SWIRLS

If passion fruit is not available, this simple dessert can be made with raspberries alone.

INGREDIENTS

Serves 4

300g/11oz/2½ cups raspberries
2 passion fruit
400g/14oz/1⅔ cups low fat fromage frais
30ml/2 tbsp caster sugar
raspberries and sprigs of mint, to decorate

1 Mash the raspberries in a small bowl with a fork until the juice runs. Scoop out the passion fruit pulp into a separate bowl with the fromage frais and sugar and mix well.

2 Spoon alternate spoonfuls of the raspberry pulp and the fromage frais mixture into stemmed glasses or one large serving dish, stirring lightly to create a swirled effect.

3 Decorate each dessert with a whole raspberry and a sprig of fresh mint. Serve chilled.

COOK'S TIP
Over-ripe, slightly soft fruit can also be used in this recipe. Use frozen raspberries when fresh are not available, but thaw first.

NUTRITION NOTES	
Per portion:	
Energy	110Kcals/462kJ
Fat	0.47g
Saturated fat	0.13g
Cholesterol	1mg
Fibre	2.12g

RED BERRY SPONGE TART

When soft berry fruits are in season, try making this delicious sponge tart. Serve warm from the oven with scoops of low fat vanilla ice cream, if you wish.

NUTRITION NOTES

Per portion:
Energy	219Kcals/919kJ
Fat	11.31g
Saturated fat	2.05g
Cholesterol	112.6mg
Fibre	4.49g

INGREDIENTS

Serves 4

softened butter, for greasing
450g/1 lb/4 cups soft berry fruits such as raspberries, blackberries, blackcurrants, redcurrants, strawberries or blueberries
2 eggs, at room temperature
50g/2oz/¼ cup caster sugar, plus extra to taste (optional)
15ml/1 tbsp plain flour
25g/1oz/¼ cup ground almonds
vanilla ice cream, to serve (optional)

VARIATION
When berry fruits are out of season, use bottled fruits, but ensure that they are very well drained before use.

1 Preheat the oven to 190°C/375°F/ Gas 5. Brush a 23cm/9 in flan tin with softened butter and line the bottom with a circle of non-stick baking paper. Scatter the fruit in the base of the tin with a little sugar if the fruits are tart.

2 Whisk the eggs and sugar together for about 3–4 minutes or until they leave a thick trail across the surface. Combine the flour and almonds, then fold into the egg mixture with a spatula – retaining as much air as possible.

3 Spread the mixture on top of the fruit base and bake in the preheated oven for about 15 minutes. Turn out on to a serving plate and serve, with low fat vanilla ice cream if you like.

COOK'S TIP
Fresh soft berry fruits are best used on the day of purchase. If you purchase them in traditional punnets, avoid any badly stained containers.

RASPBERRY-PASSION FRUIT CHINCHILLAS

Few desserts are so strikingly easy to make as this one: beaten egg whites and sugar baked in a dish, turned out and served with a handful of soft fruit and ready-made custard from a carton.

INGREDIENTS

Serves 4

25g/1oz/2 tbsp butter, softened
5 egg whites
150g/5oz/⅔ cup caster sugar
2 passion fruit
675g/1½ lb/6 cups fresh raspberries
250ml/8fl oz/1 cup low fat ready-made
    custard from a carton or can
skimmed milk, as required
icing sugar, for dusting

NUTRITION NOTES

Per portion:

Energy	309Kcals/1296kJ
Fat	5.74g
Saturated fat	3.3g
Cholesterol	15.81mg
Fibre	4.47g

1 Preheat the oven to 180°C/350°F/ Gas 4. With a brush, paint four 300ml/½ pint/1¼ cup soufflé dishes with a visible layer of soft butter.

2 Whisk the egg whites in a mixing bowl until firm. (You can use an electric mixer.) Add the sugar a little at a time and whisk into a firm meringue.

3 Halve the passion fruit, take out the seeds with a spoon and fold them into the meringue.

4 Turn the meringue out into the four prepared dishes, stand them in a deep roasting tin which has been half-filled with boiling water and bake for about 10 minutes.

5 Turn the chinchillas out upside-down on to individual plates.

6 Top the chinchillas with the fresh raspberries. Thin the custard with a little skimmed milk and pour around the edge. Dredge with icing sugar and serve warm or cold.

COOK'S TIP
If raspberries are out of season, use either fresh, bottled or canned soft berry fruit such as strawberries, blueberries or redcurrants.

CAKES, BAKES AND BREADS

The main advantage of baking your own cakes and cookies is that
you can control exactly what goes into them. Most commercially
produced cakes and bakes contain a high proportion of saturated fats,
but it is possible to bake at home using less fat, different types of fat,
and often less sugar too. All the bakes in this chapter are low in fat, and
in many cases contain little or no eggs, and often sugar is reduced by
using fruits to sweeten the mixture. The main drawback is that the cakes
will not keep for nearly as long as traditional recipes, but it is a problem
far outweighed by the health advantages. So, as you fill the
cookie jar with Apricot Yogurt Cookies or serve up that luscious slice of
Carrot Cake, your conscience is clear – let them eat cake!

Spiral Herb Bread

An attractive and delicious bread which is ideal for serving with a salad for a healthy lunch.

Ingredients

Makes 2 loaves

30ml/2 tbsp easy-blend dried yeast
600ml/1 pint/2½ cups lukewarm water
425g/15oz/3⅔ cups strong white flour
500g/1¼ lb/5 cups wholemeal flour
7.5ml/3 tsp salt
25g/1oz/2 tbsp sunflower margarine
1 large bunch parsley, finely chopped
1 bunch spring onions, chopped
1 garlic clove, finely chopped
salt and black pepper
1 egg, lightly beaten
skimmed milk, for glazing

Nutrition Notes	
Per loaf:	
Energy	1698Kcals/7132kJ
Fat	24.55g
Saturated fat	9.87g
Cholesterol	144.33mg
Fibre	30.96g

1 Combine the yeast with approximately 50ml/2fl oz/¼ cup of the water, stir and leave to dissolve.

2 Mix together the flours and salt in a large bowl. Make a well in the centre and pour in the yeast mixture and the remaining water. With a wooden spoon, stir from the centre, working outwards to obtain a rough dough.

3 Transfer the dough to a floured surface and knead until smooth and elastic. Return to the bowl, cover with a plastic bag, and leave for about 2 hours until doubled in volume.

4 Meanwhile, combine the margarine, parsley, spring onions and garlic in a large frying pan. Cook over a low heat, stirring, until softened. Season and set aside.

5 Grease two 23 x 13cm/9 x 5 in loaf tins. When the dough has risen, cut in half and roll each half into a rectangle about 35 x 23cm/14 x 9 in.

6 Brush both with the beaten egg. Divide the herb mixture between the two, spreading just up to the edges.

7 Roll up to enclose the filling and pinch the short ends to seal. Place in the tins, seam-side down.

8 Cover the dough with a clean dish towel and leave undisturbed in a warm place until the dough rises above the rim of the tins.

9 Preheat the oven to 190°C/375°F/ Gas 5. Brush the loaves with milk and bake for about 55 minutes until the bottoms sound hollow when tapped. Cool on a wire rack.

WALNUT BREAD

Delicious at any time of day, this bread may be eaten plain or topped with some low fat cream cheese.

INGREDIENTS

Makes 1 loaf

425g/15oz/3¾ cups wholemeal flour
150g/5oz/1¼ cups strong white flour
12.5ml/2½ tsp salt
525ml/18fl oz/2¼ cups lukewarm water
15ml/1 tbsp clear honey
15ml/1 tbsp easy-blend dried yeast
150g/5oz/1¼ cups walnut pieces, plus
*   more for decorating*
1 egg, beaten, for glazing

NUTRITION NOTES

Per loaf:
Energy	2852Kcals/11980kJ
Fat	109.34g
Saturated fat	12.04g
Cholesterol	77mg
Fibre	47.04g

1 Mix together the flours and salt in a large bowl. Make a well in the centre and pour in 250ml/8fl oz/1 cup of the water, the honey and the yeast.

2 Set aside until the yeast dissolves and the mixture is frothy.

3 Add the remaining water. With a wooden spoon, stir from the centre, incorporating flour with each turn, to obtain a smooth dough. Add more flour if the dough is too sticky and use your hands if the dough becomes too stiff to stir.

4 Transfer to a floured board and knead, adding flour if necessary, until the dough is smooth and elastic. Place in a greased bowl and roll the dough around in the bowl to coat thoroughly all over.

5 Cover with a plastic bag and leave in a warm place until doubled in volume, about 1½ hours.

6 Punch down the dough very firmly and knead in the walnuts until they are evenly distributed.

7 Grease a baking sheet. Shape the dough into a round loaf and place on the baking sheet. Press in the walnut pieces to decorate the top. Cover the dough loosely with a damp dish towel and leave in a warm place for about 25–30 minutes until doubled in size.

8 Preheat the oven to 220°C/425°F/ Gas 7. With a sharp knife, score the top of the loaf and brush with the egg glaze. Bake for 15 minutes. Lower the temperature to 190°C/375°F/Gas 5 and bake until the bottom of the loaf sounds hollow when tapped, about 40 minutes. Leave to cool.

OATMEAL BREAD

A healthy bread, with a delightfully crumbly texture due to the inclusion of rolled oats.

INGREDIENTS

Makes 2 loaves
475ml/16fl oz/2 cups skimmed milk
25g/1oz/2 tbsp low fat margarine
50g/2oz/1¼ cups dark brown sugar
10ml/2 tsp salt
15ml/1 tbsp easy-blend dried yeast
50ml/2fl oz/¼ cup lukewarm water
400g/14oz/3½ cups rolled oats
450–675g/1–1½ lb/4–6 cups strong white flour

1 Scald the milk. Remove from the heat and stir in the margerine, sugar and salt. Leave until lukewarm.

2 Combine the yeast and lukewarm water in a large bowl and leave until the yeast is dissolved and the mixture is frothy. Stir in the milk mixture.

3 Add 275g/10oz/2½ cups of the oats and enough flour to obtain a soft pliable dough.

4 Transfer to a floured surface and knead until smooth and elastic.

5 Place the dough in a greased bowl, cover with a plastic bag, and leave it for about 2–3 hours, until doubled in volume. Grease a large baking sheet.

6 Transfer the dough to a lightly floured surface and divide in half.

7 Shape into rounds. Place on the baking sheet, cover with a damp dish towel and leave to rise for about 1 hour, until doubled in volume.

8 Preheat the oven to 200°C/400°F/ Gas 6. Score the tops of the loaves and sprinkle with the remaining oats. Bake for about 45–50 minutes, until the bottoms sound hollow when tapped. Cool on wire racks.

NUTRITION NOTES

Per loaf:
Energy	2281Kcals/9581kJ
Fat	34.46g
Saturated fat	11.94g
Cholesterol	39mg
Fibre	24.11g

APRICOT AND ORANGE ROULADE

This elegant dessert is very good served with a spoonful of natural yogurt or crème fraîche.

INGREDIENTS

Serves 6
4 egg whites
115g/4oz/½ cup golden caster sugar
50g/2oz/½ cup plain flour
finely grated rind of 1 small orange
45ml/3 tbsp orange juice
10ml/2 tsp icing sugar and shreds of
   orange zest, to decorate

For the filling
115g/4oz/⅔ cup ready-to-eat dried
  apricots
150ml/¼ pint/⅔ cup orange juice

NUTRITION NOTES

Per portion:
Energy	203Kcals/853kJ
Fat	10.52g
Saturated fat	2.05g
Cholesterol	0
Fibre	2.53g

1 Preheat the oven to 200°C/400°F/ Gas 6. Grease a 23 x 33cm/9 x 13 in Swiss roll tin and line it with non-stick baking paper. Grease the paper.

2 For the roulade, place the egg whites in a large bowl and whisk them until they hold soft peaks. Gradually add the sugar, whisking hard between each addition.

3 Fold in the flour, orange rind and juice. Spoon the mixture into the prepared tin and spread it evenly.

4 Bake for about 15–18 minutes, or until the sponge is firm and light golden in colour. Turn out on to a sheet of non-stick baking paper and roll it up Swiss roll-style loosely from one short side. Leave to cool.

5 For the filling, roughly chop the apricots, and place them in a saucepan with the orange juice. Cover the pan and leave to simmer until most of the liquid has been absorbed. Purée the apricots in a food processor or blender.

6 Unroll the roulade and spread with the apricot mixture. Roll up, arrange strips of paper diagonally across the roll, sprinkle lightly with lines of icing sugar, remove the paper and scatter with orange zest to serve.

COOK'S TIP
Make and bake the sponge mixture a day in advance and keep it, rolled with the paper, in a cool place. Fill it with the fruit purée 2–3 hours before serving. The sponge can also be frozen for up to 2 months; thaw it at room temperature and fill it as above.

GREEK HONEY AND LEMON CAKE

INGREDIENTS

Makes 16 slices
40g/1½oz/3 tbsp sunflower margarine
60ml/4 tbsp clear honey
finely grated rind and juice of 1 lemon
150ml/¼ pint/⅔ cup skimmed milk
150g/5oz/1¼ cups plain flour
7.5ml/1½ tsp baking powder
2.5ml/½ tsp grated nutmeg
50g/2oz/¼ cup semolina
2 egg whites
10ml/2 tsp sesame seeds

1 Preheat the oven to 200°C/400°F/ Gas 6. Lightly oil a 19cm/7½in square deep cake tin (pan) and line the base with non-stick baking paper.

2 Place the margarine and 45ml/3 tbsp of the honey in a saucepan and heat gently until melted. Reserve 15ml/1 tbsp lemon juice, then stir in the rest with the lemon rind and milk.

3 Sift together the flour, baking powder and nutmeg, then beat in with the semolina. Whisk the egg whites until they form soft peaks, then fold evenly into the mixture.

4 Spoon into the tin and sprinkle with sesame seeds. Bake for 25–30 minutes, until golden brown. Mix the reserved honey and lemon juice and drizzle over the cake while warm. Cool in the tin, then cut into fingers to serve.

NUTRITION NOTES

Per portion:
Energy	82Kcals/342kJ
Fat	2.62g
Saturated fat	0.46g
Cholesterol	0.36mg
Fibre	0.41g

STRAWBERRY ROULADE

INGREDIENTS

Serves 6
4 egg whites
115g/4oz/⅔ cup golden caster sugar
75g/3oz/¾ cup plain flour
30ml/2 tbsp orange juice
115g/4oz/1 cup strawberries, chopped
150g/5oz/¼ cup low fat fromage frais
caster sugar, for sprinkling
strawberries, to decorate

1 Preheat the oven to 200°C/400°F/ Gas 6. Oil a 23 x 33cm/9 x 13in Swiss roll tin and line with non-stick baking paper.

2 Place the egg whites in a large bowl and whisk until they form soft peaks. Gradually whisk in the sugar. Fold in half of the sifted flour, then fold in the rest with the orange juice.

3 Spoon the mixture into the prepared tin, spreading evenly. Bake for 15-18 minutes, or until golden brown and firm to the touch.

4 Meanwhile, spread out a sheet of non-stick baking paper and sprinkle with caster sugar. Turn out the cake on to this and remove the lining paper. Roll up the sponge loosely from one short side, with the paper inside. Cool.

5 Unroll and remove the paper. Stir the strawberries into the fromage frais and spread over the sponge. Reroll and serve decorated with strawberries.

NUTRITION NOTES

Per portion:
Energy	154Kcals/646kJ
Fat	0.24g
Saturated fat	0.05g
Cholesterol	0.25mg
Fibre	0.6g

SAGE SODA BREAD

This wonderful loaf, quite unlike bread made with yeast, has a velvety texture and a powerful sage aroma.

INGREDIENTS

Makes 1 loaf
225g/8oz/1½ cups wholemeal flour
115g/4oz/1 cup strong white flour
2.5ml/½ tsp salt
5ml/1 tsp bicarbonate of soda
30ml/2 tbsp shredded fresh sage or
   10ml/2 tsp dried sage
300–450ml/½–¾ pint/1¼–1¾ cups
   buttermilk

VARIATION
As an alternative to the sage, try using either finely chopped rosemary or thyme.

NUTRITION NOTES

Per loaf:
Energy	1251Kcals/5255kJ
Fat	9.23g
Saturated fat	2g
Cholesterol	7mg
Fibre	23.81g

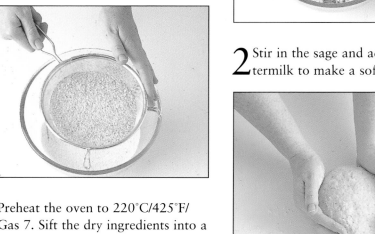

1 Preheat the oven to 220°C/425°F/ Gas 7. Sift the dry ingredients into a mixing bowl.

2 Stir in the sage and add enough buttermilk to make a soft dough.

3 Shape the dough into a round loaf with your hands and place on a lightly oiled baking sheet.

4 Cut a deep cross in the top. Bake in the oven for about 40 minutes until the loaf is well risen and sounds hollow when tapped on the bottom. Leave to cool on a wire rack.

COURGETTE AND WALNUT LOAF

INGREDIENTS

Makes 1 loaf

3 eggs
75g/3oz/½ cup light brown sugar
50ml/2fl oz/¼ cup sunflower oil
225g/8oz/1½ cups wholemeal flour
5ml/1 tsp baking powder
5ml/1 tsp bicarbonate of soda
5ml/1 tsp ground cinnamon
2.5ml/½ tsp ground allspice
7.5ml/½ tbsp green cardamoms, seeds
  removed and crushed
150g/5oz/1 cup coarsely grated
  courgette
50g/2oz/¼ cup walnuts, chopped
50g/2oz/¼ cup sunflower seeds

NUTRITION NOTES

Per portion:

Energy	3073Kcals/12908kJ
Fat	201.98g
Saturated fat	26.43g
Cholesterol	654.5mg
Fibre	28.62g

1 Preheat the oven to 180°C/350°F/ Gas 4. Grease the base and sides of a 900g/2 lb loaf tin and line with greaseproof paper.

2 Beat the eggs and sugar together and gradually add the oil.

3 Sift the flour into a bowl together with the baking powder, bicarbonate of soda, cinnamon and allspice.

4 Mix into the egg mixture with the rest of the ingredients, reserving 15ml/1 tbsp of the sunflower seeds for the top.

5 Spoon into the loaf tin, level off the top, and sprinkle with the reserved sunflower seeds.

6 Bake for about 1 hour or until a skewer inserted in the centre comes out clean. Leave to cool slightly, then turn out on to a wire cooling rack.

SAFFRON FOCCACIA

A dazzling yellow bread with a distinctive flavour.

INGREDIENTS

Makes 1 loaf
pinch of saffron threads
150ml/¼ pint/⅔ cup boiling water
225g/8oz/2 cups plain flour
2.5ml/½ tsp salt
5ml/1 tsp easy-blend dried yeast
15ml/1 tbsp olive oil

For the topping
2 garlic cloves, sliced
1 red onion, cut into thin wedges
rosemary sprigs
12 black olives, stoned and coarsely chopped
15ml/1 tbsp olive oil

NUTRITION NOTES

Per loaf:
Energy	1047Kcals/4399kJ
Fat	29.15g
Saturated fat	4.06g
Cholesterol	0
Fibre	9.48g

1 Place the saffron in a heatproof jug and pour on the boiling water. Leave to infuse until the saffron mixture is lukewarm.

2 Place the flour, salt, yeast and olive oil in a food processor. Turn on and gradually add the saffron and its liquid until the dough forms a ball.

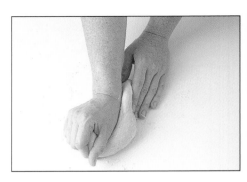

3 Turn out on to a floured board and knead for 10–15 minutes. Place in a bowl, cover and leave to rise for about 30–40 minutes, until doubled in size.

4 Punch down the risen dough on a lightly floured surface and roll out into an oval shape, 1cm/½ in thick. Place on a lightly greased baking sheet and leave to rise for 20–30 minutes.

5 Preheat the oven to 200°C/400°F/ Gas 6. Use your fingers to press small indentations in the dough.

6 Cover with the topping ingredients, brush lightly with olive oil, and bake for about 25 minutes or until the loaf sounds hollow when tapped on the bottom. Leave to cool.

TOMATO BREADSTICKS

Once you've tried this simple recipe you'll never buy manufactured breadsticks again. Serve as a snack, or with aperitifs and a dip at the beginning of a meal.

INGREDIENTS

Makes 16
225g/8oz/2 cups plain flour
2.5ml/½ tsp salt
2.5ml/½ tbsp easy-blend dry yeast
5ml/1 tsp honey
5ml/1 tsp olive oil
150ml/¼ pint/⅔ cup warm water
6 halves sun-dried tomatoes in olive oil, drained and chopped
15ml/1 tbsp skimmed milk
10ml/2 tsp poppy seeds

NUTRITION NOTES

Per portion:
Energy	82Kcals/346kJ
Fat	3.53g
Saturated fat	0.44g
Cholesterol	0
Fibre	0.44g

1 Place the flour, salt and yeast in a food processor. Add the honey and olive oil and, with the machine running, gradually pour in the water (you may not need it all as flours vary). Stop adding water as soon as the dough starts to cling together. Process for 1 minute more.

2 Turn out the dough on to a floured board and knead for 3–4 minutes until springy and smooth.

3 Knead in the chopped sun-dried tomatoes. Form into a ball and place in a lightly oiled bowl. Leave to rise for 5 minutes.

4 Preheat the oven to 150°C/300°F/Gas 2. Divide the dough into sixteen pieces and roll each piece into a 28 x 1cm/11 x ½ in long stick. Place on a lightly oiled baking sheet and leave to rise in a warm place for 15 minutes.

5 Brush the sticks with milk and sprinkle with poppy seeds. Bake for 30 minutes. Leave to cool on a wire cooling rack.

VARIATION
Instead of sun-dried tomatoes, you could try making these breadsticks with reduced fat Cheddar cheese, sesame seeds or herbs.

CHERRY MARMALADE MUFFINS

INGREDIENTS

Makes 12

225g/8oz/2 cups self-raising flour
5ml/1 tsp ground mixed spice
75g/3oz/6 tbsp caster sugar
115g/4oz/½ cup glacé cherries,
    quartered
30ml/2 tbsp orange marmalade
150ml/¼ pint/⅔ cup skimmed milk
50g/2oz/4 tbsp soft sunflower
    margarine
marmalade, to brush

1 Preheat the oven to 200°C/400°F/
Gas 6. Lightly grease 12 deep
muffin tins with oil.

2 Sift together the flour and spice
then stir in the sugar and cherries.

3 Mix the marmalade with the milk
and beat into the dry ingredients
with the margarine. Spoon into the
greased tins. Bake for 20–25 minutes,
until golden brown and firm.

4 Turn out on to a wire rack and
brush the tops with warmed
marmalade. Serve warm or cold.

NUTRITION NOTES

Per portion:
Energy	154Kcals/650kJ
Fat	3.66g
Saturated fat	0.68g
Cholesterol	0.54mg
Fibre	0.69g

FRUIT SALAD CAKE

INGREDIENTS

Makes 1 cake

175g/6oz/¾ cup roughly chopped dried
    fruit salad mixture, e.g. apples, apri-
    cots, prunes and peaches
250ml/8 fl oz/1 cup hot tea
225g/8oz/2 cups wholemeal self-raising
    flour
5ml/1 tsp grated nutmeg
50g/2oz/4 tbsp dark muscovado sugar
45ml/3 tbsp sunflower oil
45ml/3 tbsp skimmed milk
demerara sugar, to sprinkle

NUTRITION NOTES

Per cake:
Energy	1615Kcals/6786kJ
Fat	39.93g
Saturated fat	5.22g
Cholesterol	0.9mg
Fibre	31.12g

1 Soak the dried fruits in the tea for
several hours or overnight. Drain
and reserve the liquid.

2 Preheat the oven to 180°C/350°F/
Gas 4. Grease an 18cm/7 in round
cake tin and line the base with non-
stick baking paper.

3 Sift the flour into a bowl with the
nutmeg. Stir in the muscovado
sugar, fruit and tea. Add the oil and
milk and mix well.

4 Spoon the mixture into the prepared
tin and sprinkle with demerara
sugar. Bake for 50–55 minutes or until
firm. Turn out and cool on a wire rack.

BANANA GINGER PARKIN

Parkin keeps well and really improves with keeping. Store it in a covered container for up to two months.

INGREDIENTS

Makes 1 cake
200g/7oz/1¼ cups plain flour
10ml/2 tsp bicarbonate of soda
10ml/2 tsp ground ginger
150g/5oz/1¼ cups medium oatmeal
60ml/4 tbsp dark muscovado sugar
75g/3oz/6 tbsp sunflower margarine
150g/5oz/⅔ cup golden syrup
1 egg, beaten
3 ripe bananas, mashed
75g/3oz/¾ cup icing sugar
stem ginger, to decorate

1 Preheat the oven to 160°C/325°F/ Gas 3. Grease and line an 18 x 28cm/7 x 11in cake tin.

2 Sift together the flour, bicarbonate of soda and ginger, then stir in the oatmeal. Melt the sugar, margarine and syrup in a saucepan, then stir into the flour mixture. Beat in the egg and mashed bananas.

3 Spoon into the tin and bake for about 1 hour, or until firm to the touch. Allow to cool in the tin, then turn out and cut into squares.

4 Sift the icing sugar into a bowl and stir in just enough water to make a smooth, runny icing. Drizzle the icing over each square and top with a piece of stem ginger, if you like.

COOK'S TIP
This is a nutritious, energy-giving cake that is a really good choice for packed lunches as it doesn't break up too easily.

NUTRITION NOTES	
Per cake:	
Energy	3320Kcals/13946kJ
Fat	83.65g
Saturated fat	16.34g
Cholesterol	197.75mg
Fibre	20.69g

SPICED DATE AND WALNUT CAKE

A classic flavour combination, which makes a very easy low fat, high-fibre cake.

INGREDIENTS

Makes 1 cake
*300g/11oz/2½ cups wholemeal self-
raising flour*
10ml/2 tsp mixed spice
150g/5oz/¾ cup chopped dates
50g/2oz/½ cup chopped walnuts
60ml/4 tbsp sunflower oil
115g/4oz/½ cup dark muscovado sugar
300ml/½ pint/1¼ cups skimmed milk
walnut halves, to decorate

1 Preheat the oven to 180°C/350°F/ Gas 4. Grease and line a 900g/2 lb loaf tin with greaseproof paper.

2 Sift together the flour and spice, adding back any bran from the sieve. Stir in the dates and walnuts.

3 Mix the oil, sugar and milk, then stir evenly into the dry ingredients. Spoon into the prepared tin and arrange the walnut halves on top.

4 Bake the cake in the oven for about 45–50 minutes, or until golden brown and firm. Turn out the cake, remove the lining paper and leave to cool on a wire rack.

NUTRITION NOTES

· Per cake:

Energy	2654Kcals/11146kJ
Fat	92.78g
Saturated fat	11.44g
Cholesterol	6mg
Fibre	35.1g

COOK'S TIP
Pecan nuts can be used in place of the walnuts in this cake.

SUNFLOWER SULTANA SCONES

INGREDIENTS

Makes 10–12

225g/8oz/2 cups self-raising flour
5ml/1 tsp baking powder
25g/1oz/2 tbsp soft sunflower
  margarine
30ml/2 tbsp golden caster sugar
50g/2oz/⅓ cup sultanas
30ml/2 tbsp sunflower seeds
150g/5oz/⅔ cup natural yogurt
about 30–45ml/2–3 tbsp skimmed milk

1 Preheat the oven to 230°C/450°F/ Gas 8. Lightly oil a baking sheet. Sift the flour and baking powder into a bowl and rub in the margarine evenly.

2 Stir in the sugar, sultanas and half the sunflower seeds, then mix in the yogurt, with just enough milk to make a fairly soft, but not sticky dough.

3 Roll out on a lightly floured surface to about 2cm/¾ in thickness. Cut into 6cm/2½ in flower shapes or rounds with a biscuit cutter and lift on to the baking sheet.

4 Brush with milk and sprinkle with the reserved sunflower seeds, then bake for 10–12 minutes, until well risen and golden brown.

5 Cool the scones on a wire rack. Serve split and spread with jam or low fat spread.

NUTRITION NOTES

Per portion:

Energy	176Kcals/742kJ
Fat	5.32g
Saturated fat	0.81g
Cholesterol	0.84mg
Fibre	1.26g

PRUNE AND PEEL ROCK BUNS

INGREDIENTS

Makes 12

225g/8oz/2 cups plain flour
10ml/2 tsp baking powder
75g/3oz/⅔ cup demerara sugar
50g/2oz/½ cup chopped ready-to-eat
  dried prunes
50g/2oz/⅓ cup chopped mixed peel
finely grated rind of 1 lemon
50ml/2 fl oz/¼ cup sunflower oil
75ml/5 tbsp skimmed milk

NUTRITION NOTES

Per portion:

Energy	135Kcals/570kJ
Fat	3.35g
Saturated fat	0.44g
Cholesterol	0.13mg
Fibre	0.86g

1 Preheat the oven to 200°C/400°F/ Gas 6. Lightly oil a large baking sheet. Sift together the flour and baking powder, then stir in the sugar, prunes, peel and lemon rind.

2 Mix the oil and milk, then stir into the mixture, to make a dough which just binds together.

3 Spoon into rocky heaps on the baking sheet and bake for 20 minutes, until golden. Cool on a wire rack.

BANANA ORANGE LOAF

For the best banana flavour and a really good, moist texture, make sure the bananas are very ripe for this cake.

INGREDIENTS

Makes 1 loaf
90g/3½oz/¾ cup wholemeal plain flour
90g/3½oz/¾ cup plain flour
5ml/1 tsp baking powder
5ml/1 tsp ground mixed spice
45ml/3 tbsp flaked hazelnuts, toasted
2 large ripe bananas
1 egg
30ml/2 tbsp sunflower oil
30ml/2 tbsp clear honey
finely grated rind and juice 1 small orange
4 orange slices, halved
10ml/2 tsp icing sugar

1 Preheat the oven to 180°C/350°F/ Gas 4. Brush a 1 litre/1¾ pint/4 cup loaf tin with sunflower oil and line the base with non-stick baking paper.

2 Sift the flour with the baking powder and spice into a large bowl, adding any bran that is caught in the sieve. Stir the hazelnuts into the dry ingredients.

3 Peel and mash the bananas. Beat in the egg, oil, honey and the orange rind and juice. Stir evenly into the dry ingredients.

4 Spoon into the prepared tin and smooth the top. Bake for 40–45 minutes, or until firm and golden brown. Turn out and cool on a wire rack to cool.

5 Sprinkle the orange slices with the icing sugar and grill until golden. Use to decorate the cake.

COOK'S TIP
If you plan to keep the loaf for more than two or three days, omit the orange slices, brush with honey and sprinkle with flaked hazelnuts.

NUTRITION NOTES

Per cake:

Energy	1741Kcals/7314kJ
Fat	60.74g
Saturated fat	7.39g
Cholesterol	192.5mg
Fibre	19.72g

APRICOT YOGURT COOKIES

These soft cookies are very quick to make and are useful for the biscuit tin or for lunch boxes.

— INGREDIENTS —

Makes 16

175g/6oz/1½ cups plain flour
5ml/1 tsp baking powder
5ml/1 tsp ground cinnamon
75g/3oz/1 cup rolled oats
75g/3oz/½ cup light muscovado sugar
115g/4oz/½ cup chopped ready-to-eat dried apricots
15ml/1 tbsp flaked hazelnuts or almonds
150g/5oz/⅔ cup natural yogurt
45ml/3 tbsp sunflower oil
demerara sugar, to sprinkle

1 Preheat the oven to 190°C/375°F/ Gas 5. Lightly oil a large baking sheet.

2 Sift together the flour, baking powder and cinnamon. Stir in the oats, sugar, apricots and nuts.

3 Beat together the yogurt and oil, then stir evenly into the mixture to make a firm dough. If necessary, add a little more yogurt.

4 Use your hands to roll the mixture into about 16 small balls, place on the baking sheet and flatten with a fork.

5 Sprinkle with demerara sugar. Bake for 15–20 minutes, or until firm and golden brown. Leave to cool on a wire rack.

COOK'S TIP
These cookies do not keep well, so it is best to eat them within two days, or to freeze them. Pack into polythene bags and freeze for up to four months.

— NUTRITION NOTES —

Per portion:
Energy	95Kcals/400kJ
Fat	2.66g
Saturated fat	0.37g
Cholesterol	0.3mg
Fibre	0.94g

EGGLESS CHRISTMAS CAKE

INGREDIENTS

Makes 1x18cm/7in square cake
75g/3oz/⅔ cup sultanas
75g/3oz/⅔ cup raisins
75g/3oz/½ cup currants
75g/3oz/⅓ cup glacé cherries, halved
50g/2oz/¼ cup cut mixed peel
250ml/8 fl oz/1 cup apple juice
25g/1oz/¼ cup toasted hazelnuts
30ml/2 tbsp pumpkin seeds
2 pieces stem ginger in syrup, chopped
finely grated rind of 1 lemon
120ml/4 fl oz/½ cup skimmed milk
50ml/2 fl oz/¼ cup sunflower oil
*225g/8oz/1¼ cups wholemeal self-
    raising flour*
10ml/2 tsp mixed spice
45ml/3 tbsp brandy or dark rum
apricot jam, for brushing
glacé fruits, to decorate

1 Place the sultanas, raisins, currants, cherries and peel in a bowl and stir in the apple juice. Cover and leave to soak overnight.

2 Preheat the oven to 150°C/300°F/ Gas 2. Grease and line an 18cm/7in square cake tin.

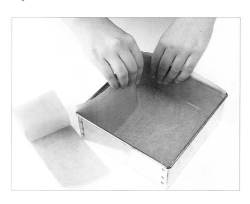

3 Add the hazelnuts, pumpkin seeds, ginger and lemon rind to the soaked fruit. Stir in the milk and oil. Sift the flour and spice and stir into the mixture with the brandy or rum.

4 Spoon into the prepared tin and bake for about 1½ hours, or until the cake is golden brown and firm to the touch.

5 Turn out and cool on a wire rack. Brush with sieved apricot jam and decorate with glacé fruits.

NUTRITION NOTES	
Per cake:	
Energy	2702Kcals/11352kJ
Fat	73.61g
Saturated fat	10.69g
Cholesterol	2.4mg
Fibre	29.46g

CRANBERRY AND APPLE RING

Tangy cranberries add an unusual flavour to this low fat cake. It is best eaten very fresh.

INGREDIENTS

Makes 1 ring cake
225g/8oz/2 cups self-raising flour
5ml/1 tsp ground cinnamon
75g/3oz/½ cup light muscovado sugar
1 crisp eating apple, cored and diced
75g/3oz/⅔ cup fresh or frozen
cranberries
60ml/4 tbsp sunflower oil
150ml/¼ pint/⅔ cup apple juice
cranberry jelly and apple slices, to
decorate

1 Preheat the oven to 180°C/350°F/ Gas 4. Lightly grease a 1 litre/1¼ pint/4 cup ring tin with oil.

2 Sift together the flour and ground cinnamon, then stir in the sugar.

3 Toss together the diced apple and cranberries. Stir into the dry ingredients, then add the oil and apple juice and beat well.

4 Spoon the mixture into the prepared ring tin and bake for about 35–40 minutes, or until the cake is firm to the touch. Turn out and leave to cool completely on a wire rack.

5 To serve, drizzle warmed cranberry jelly over the cake and decorate with apple slices.

COOK'S TIP
Fresh cranberries are available throughout the winter months and if you don't use them all at once, they can be frozen for up to a year.

NUTRITION NOTES

Per cake:

Energy	1616Kcals/6787kJ
Fat	47.34g
Saturated fat	6.14g
Cholesterol	0
Fibre	12.46g

CARROT CAKE WITH LEMON FROSTING

INGREDIENTS

Makes one 18cm/7in cake
225g/8oz/1¼ cups wholemeal self-
raising flour
10ml/2 tsp ground allspice
115g/4oz/⅔ cup light muscovado
sugar
3 medium carrots (about 225g/8oz),
grated
50g/2oz/⅓ cup sultanas
75ml/5 tbsp sunflower oil
75ml/5 tbsp orange juice
75ml/5 tbsp skimmed milk
2 egg whites

For the frosting
175g/6oz/¾ cup skimmed milk soft
cheese
finely grated rind of ½ lemon
30ml/2 tbsp clear honey
shreds of lemon rind, to decorate

1 Preheat the oven to 180°C/350°F/
Gas 4. Grease a deep 18 cm/7in
round cake tin and line the base with
non-stick baking paper.

2 Sift the flour and spice, then stir in
the sugar, grated carrots and
sultanas. Mix the oil, orange juice and
milk, then stir evenly into the dry
ingredients. Whisk the egg whites until
stiff, then fold in lightly and evenly.

3 Spoon into the tin and bake for
45–50 minutes, until firm and golden.
Turn out and cool on a wire rack.

4 For the frosting, beat together the
cheese, lemon rind and honey until
smooth. Spread over the top of the
cooled cake, swirling with a palette
knife. Decorate the top with shreds of
lemon rind.

NUTRITION NOTES

Per cake:
Energy	2182Kcals/9167kJ
Fat	61.79g
Saturated fat	8.37g
Cholesterol	3.25mg
Fibre	26.65g

CHEWY FRUIT MUESLI SLICE

INGREDIENTS

Makes 8 slices
75g/3oz/½ cup ready-to-eat dried
apricots, chopped
1 eating apple, cored and grated
150g/5oz/1¼ cups Swiss-style muesli
150ml/¼ pint/⅔ cup apple juice
15g/½ oz/1 tbsp soft sunflower
margarine

1 Preheat the oven to 190°C/375°F/
Gas 5. Place all the ingredients in a
large bowl and mix well.

2 Press the mixture into a 20cm/8in
round, non-stick sandwich tin and
bake for 35–40 minutes, or until lightly
browned and firm.

3 Mark the muesli slice into wedges
and leave to cool in the tin.

NUTRITION NOTES

Per portion::
Energy	112Kcals/467kJ
Fat	2.75g
Saturated fat	0.48g
Cholesterol	0.13mg
Fibre	2.09g

INDEX

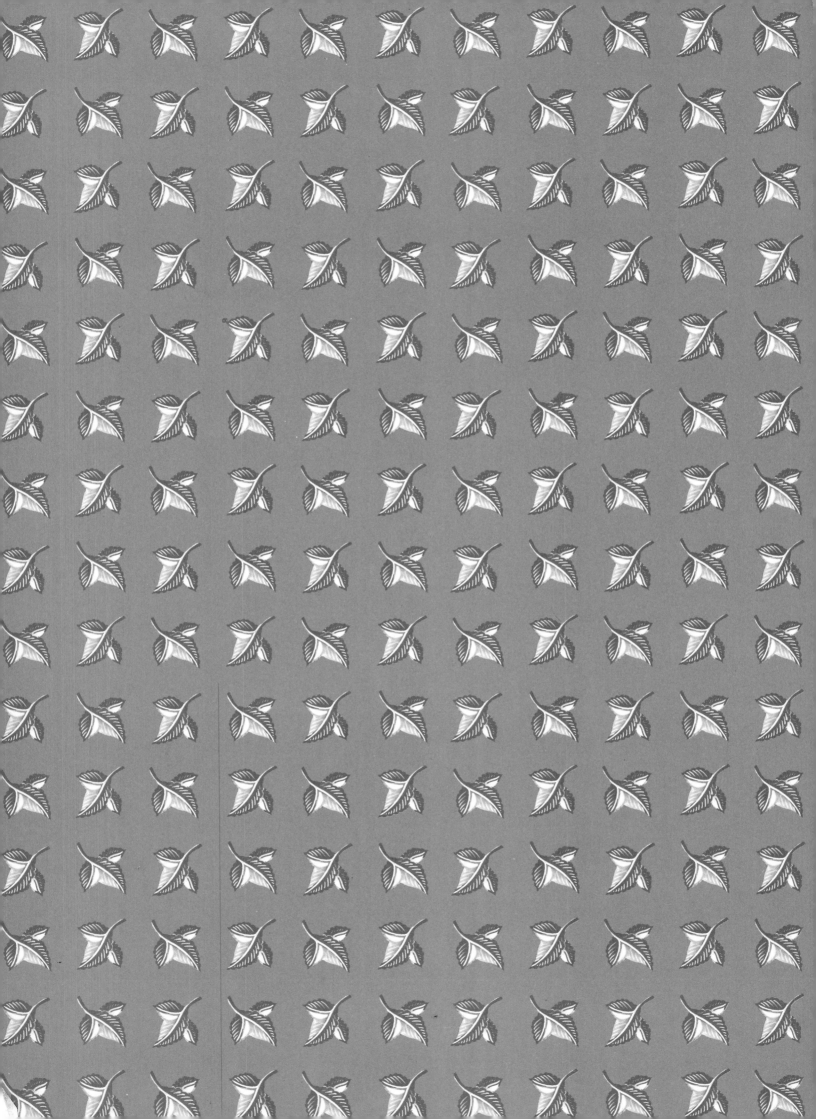